The Gift of Purpose:
Orienting the Christian Life in Western Culture

Volume 1 of God's Gifts for the Christian Life – Part 3

J. Alexander Rutherford

Unless otherwise indicated, all Scripture quotations are from The Holy Bible, English Standard Version® (ESV®), copyright © 2001 by Crossway Bibles, a publishing ministry of Good News Publishers. Used by permission. All rights reserved.

Unless otherwise indicated, all Scripture quotations from the book of Habakkuk or those marked Teleioteti are my own translations. Translations from Habakkuk are taken from the translation published in my commentary on Habakkuk (Vancouver, Teleioteti 2020).

ISBN-13: 978-1-989560-04-4

Copyright © 2020 J. Alexander Rutherford
Teleioteti publishing, Airdrie AB
All rights reserved.

To contact Teleioteti publishing for information or to provide feedback, please visit us at **https://teleioteti.ca** or email us at **info@teleioteti.ca**.

DEDICATION

Though we have now moved across the world, Nicole and I spent the first five years of our marriage with the same church community. God provided faithful friends and church family to support and sustain us throughout our marriage. This book is dedicated to our wonderful church family of the last five years, The Bridge Community Church, which has become Christ City Church Kitsilano. You were there to support us as we entered marriage and throughout my studies at Regent. This book is particularly dedicated to the group of guys who challenged me in my life and marriage and nourished my faith during that season of life. To Fred, Jordan, Stephen, Doug, and Doug, though we have often differed on our answers to the question at the heart of this book, I hope you will recognise your hand in shaping what is good and true in my writing.

CONTENTS

Dedication iii

Contents v

Series Introduction vii

Introduction 1

Part 1 - Did Christianity Save the West? 9

    Chapter 1 - Western Culture 11

    Chapter 2 - Biblically Influenced Culture 19

    Chapter 3 - Did Christianity Save the West? 25

Part 2 - Should Christianity Save the Western World? 33

    Chapter 4 - Strategies to Save the West 35

    Chapter 5 - We Save the West By Transforming It 43

    Chapter 6 - We Live in the West as Good Citizens 53

Part 3 - Loving the West Enough to Watch It Burn 69

    Chapter 7 - Ecclesiology: Fundamental Allegiance 71

    Chapter 8 - Soteriology: Redemptive Insurgency 85

    Chapter 9 - Eschatology: Exilic Life 111

    Conclusion 119

Part 4 - Appendices **123**
    Appendix 1: Review of Empires of Dirt 125
    Appendix 2: Review of The Case for Classical Christian Education 133
    Appendix 3: Review of The City of God and the Goal of Creation. 141
    Appendix 4: Review of Living in God's Two Kingdoms 145
    Bibliography 155
    About Teleioteti 161
        Other Books by J. Alexander Rutherford 162

SERIES INTRODUCTION

> His divine power has granted to us all things that pertain to life and godliness, through the knowledge of him who called us to his own glory and excellence. – 1 Peter 3:3

God has not left His people without help in the day of trouble—or in the day of prosperity for that matter. The Bible is God's gift to His people, revealing to them Jesus Christ and the salvation He has accomplished. But the gift of Scripture does not end in revealing our need for salvation and God's provision for it; Scripture is sufficient for the entire Christian life. In his first epistle, Peter tells us that God's divine power has given us everything for life and godliness (1 Pet 3:3, cf. 2 Tim 3:16-17).

In *God's Gifts for the Christian Life*, J. Alexander Rutherford unpacks how God through the Bible has given what we need to live faithfully in His world. Each volume unpacks the Scriptural teaching against the background of contemporary culture and shows how the Bible provides a firm foundation for our lives. Each volume is intended to be short, around 110-150 pages, and accessible to the interested reader. The primary audience is theologically interested lay-Christians (Christians who are not in paid ministry and have no formal theological training), students, and pastors.

Part 1, the Christian Mind, will address the questions raised by philosophy and culture concerning the nature and possibility of knowledge and truth. Part 2, the Christian Scriptures, will provide an overview of the Bible and its content to equip the reader for a lifelong engagement with

Scriptures and with the world Scripturally. Part 3, the Christian Life, will orient the Christian life towards culture and the church in order to show what it looks like to live a faithful, theological life. Drawing on the resources given in Parts 1 & 2, Part 3 will set forth a framework for Christians to engage intellectually with culture, life, and the local church in order to serve better within the local church context and so further God's purpose in the world.

INTRODUCTION

> We have to feel the universe at once as an ogre's castle, to be stormed, and yet as our own cottage, to which we can return at evening. – G.K. Chesterton
>
> They did not love the city enough to set fire to it. – G.K. Chesterton
>
> [Christians] live in their own homelands, but as aliens: they participate in everything as citizens but endure all things as strangers. Every foreign land is their homeland, and every homeland is foreign. – Author of *Epistle to Diognetus*

The question "Where do we belong?" is at the heart of the most significant trends in Western culture. By severing the anchor of tradition, the Enlightenment left us drifting in the vast emptiness of the universe. We found ourselves adrift, lost in space—"continually falling, and backwards, sidewards, forwards, in all directions"![1] It became quickly evident that humanity could not function as isolated islands of individuality; we longed for something to unite us. Yet we have been unable to find unity. The liberal dream of shared progress—ever upward and onward!—was shattered by two consecutive World Wars. The dream of an objective, shareable interpretation of reality was broken by the discovery that science was as subjective as the arts, involving creation as much as observation. Without a shared tradition

---

[1] Punctuation has made altered for this context. From Kaufmann's translation of Nietzsche's *The Gay Science*.

to bind us, society has fragmented at an exponential rate. In the 21st century, we have seen different identities absolutized to fill this void—gender, race, oppression, poverty, etc. The shared struggle against those with power is the only glue holding these groups and the individuals that make them up together. The fragmentation of society is not conducive to its survival; indeed, it seems to be the harbinger of its demise.

How can society function if no common ground exists? How can we share an understanding of government and social practice when we have incompatible and drastically different interpretations of God, morality, knowledge, truth, and history? This is where we find ourselves, at the edge of the precipice. Western culture appears to be in deep trouble. The solutions offered for this crisis are legion—further adding to the fragmentation. Several decades ago, there was a movement to return to theocracy as the way to mend society; here, unity would come through religious uniformity. Many still believe something similar, though not under the banner "Theonomy." Others see a return to a Judeo-Christian ethic, whether grounded in the Scriptures, Western tradition, or natural law. Among Christians, there is much debate over the general approach Christian individuals and churches should adopt towards society. Amidst those who affirm Christians should do something, the answers differ from thinker to thinker.

Christians have always wrestled with this question: how do we relate to the world—to those who are not believers and to society in general? When society is in crisis, further questions arise: should we do anything about it? What should we do about it? In a way, this book is an answer to these questions, but indirectly. I intend to equip the reader to answer these questions within their own circumstances. I intend this book to be a biblical response to the way Christians answer these questions today (Part 2) against the backdrop of Christianity's varied history with Western culture (Part 1). After this, I hope to offer some guidance to Christians asking these questions (Part 3).

I am concerned with a particular confusion I see within Conservative Christian culture. As Western culture succumbs to post-enlightenment chaos, there is a call among Conservatives and liberal Evangelicals[2] to *ressource* the

---

[2] "Liberalism" traditionally refers to a specific naturalistic interpretation of

"Great Tradition" or the "Christian Intellectual Tradition" in order to combat Postmodernism. One writer defines *ressourcement* as the act of looking "to the history of the church for resources to give theological direction to people in the twenty-first century."[3] This *ressourcement* has, in some circles, meant adopting a Platonic metaphysic and epistemology from certain early church fathers and approaching the Bible in a distinctly premodern way, namely, through allegorical interpretation.[4] Among conservatives, there has been an effort to draw on the intellectual tradition of the Fathers and medieval theologians to answer the problems of our times; this includes their philosophical, ecclesiological, and theological practices and ideas.[5] In Christian education circles, there has been a resurgence in "Classical education," a Christianised Greco-Roman model of education.[6] Some have

---

Christianity, such as was popularized by Adolf Harnack and came to dominate mainline Protestantism. "Evangelical Liberalism" is different in that it accepts a supernatural worldview, is often explicitly Trinitarian and believes in the Incarnation and even the Resurrection. However, this view is 'liberal' in that it adopts with traditional Liberal theology an unbiblical view of biblical authority, letting tradition or modern Philosophy lead the way in theology. On this broader definition of 'liberal,' cf. Francis A. Schaeffer, *The Great Evangelical Disaster* (Westchester: Crossway Books, 1984); John M. Frame, *A History of Western Philosophy and Theology* (Phillipsburg: P&R Publishing, 2015), 216–217.

[3] Hans Boersma, *Heavenly Participation: The Weaving of a Sacramental Tapestry* (Grand Rapids: Eerdmans, 2011), 9.

[4] This is characteristic of the Radical Orthodoxy movement and some schools of theological interpretation. Cf. Boersma, *Heavenly Participation*; Hans Boersma, *Sacramental Preaching: Sermons on the Hidden Presence of Christ* (Grand Rapids: Baker Academic, 2016); David C. Steinmetz, "The Superiority of Precritical Exegesis," in *A Guide to Contemporary Hermeneutics: Major Trends in biblical Interperation*, ed. Donald K. McKim (Grand Rapids: Eerdmans, 1986), 65–77.

[5] Crossway has recently launched a series for this purpose, "Reclaiming the Christian Intellectual Tradition." See my review of one of these volumes, J. Alexander Rutherford, "Review of Media, Journalism, and Communication," *Teleioteti*, May 10, 2018, accessed March 25, 2020, https://teleioteti.ca/2018/05/10/review-of-media-journalism-and-communication/.

[6] Cf. the *Case for Classic Christian Education*, the first chapters of *Christian Higher Education*, and the introduction of *Media, Communication, and Journalism*. Douglas Wilson, *The Case for Classical Christian Education* (Wheaton: Crossway Books, 2003); David S. Dockery and Christopher W. Morgan, eds., *Christian Higher Education: Faith, Teaching, and Learning in the Evangelical Tradition* (Wheaton:

suggested that we Christians need to preserve Western culture through its coming collapse, as Christian monks supposedly did after the fall of the Roman Empire.[7] Shared by the diverse authors and editors forming these streams of thought is the view that Pre-Enlightenment Western culture, with its Christianised Hellenism, provides answers to the problems of our culture. Implicit in most of this (sometimes explicit) is the idea that Western culture is something worth preserving, something Christian *ought* to preserve. I believe that these approaches in their various forms are seriously problematic. In what follows, I hope to offer a response to these trends, an argument for *Sola Scriptura* that does not reject tradition but does not privilege the ages before us as having a better handle on God's world or even God's word. Instead, we need to draw on tradition to escape the errors of our age, but we must only do so as an aid to understanding God's word. In doing so, we will escape the errors of their time. I also intend to offer a constructive proposal for faithful, Christian living in Western culture and whatever may replace it. By taking this approach, I hope that we might be able to transcend the 20th and 21st century "Christ and Culture" debate.

That is, beginning with the Niebuhr's classic, *Christ and Culture*,[8] there has been a debate over the role of Christian's within society. His categories (Christ over culture, Christ and culture in paradox, etc.) have been the point of departure for the discussion in the following decades. Even the title of this work raises some important questions. What exactly is meant by "Christ?" He does not in any straightforward fashion intend the Incarnate Son of God, who currently rules over all creation at the right hand of the Father. Niebuhr is intentionally ambiguous, but the overall discussions in which he engages suggests something like "Christianity," as in, how do Christians—does Christianity—understand what it means to live in submission to Christ in the world. By setting the discussion in terms of "*Christ* and Culture," Niebuhr

---

Crossway, 2018); Read Mercer Schuchardt, *Media, Journalism, and Communication: A Student's Guide*, Reclaiming the Christian Intellectual Tradition (Wheaton: Crossway, 2018).

[7] Gene Veith commends Rod Dreher in this regard. Gene Edward Veith, *Post Christian: A Guide to Contemporary Thought and Culture* (Wheaton: Crossway, 2020), 225–227, 277.

[8] H. Richard Niebuhr, *Christ and Culture* (New York: Harper Torchbooks, 1951).

orients the discussion around the question of Christ's lordship. Furthermore, what is meant by "culture?" How we define "culture" will shape the answer one gives to the question of Christianity's relationship to culture. Niebuhr's discussion of what he includes and excludes from culture is lengthy. Carson captures what is included in Niebuhr's definition like this: "Niebuhr's definition of culture embraces 'ideas' and 'beliefs' as well as customs, social organisation, inherited artifacts, and the like."[9] In what follows, I will loosely follow John Frame and employ the following definition of culture:

> "Culture" is used both of a shared value system within a society or group of people and the products produced by such groups ("high culture"). In the abstract, then, culture is a shared worldview, but the term "culture" is also used to refer to the embodiment of these value systems and so encompasses not just the values but also the defining physical symbols of these underlying values—political and economic systems, art, language, etc. John Frame defines culture similarly as "what human society is and what it ought to be, both real and ideal": it is a system of values defining what is 'ideal' and the imperfect embodiment of those ideals. The ideal side of culture is its worldview.[10]

Though I find value in each of the categories Niebuhr proposes, especially as discussed by D.A. Carson in his *Christ and Culture Revisited* and Timothy Keller in his *Center Church*,[11] I suspect that the manner in which Niebuhr has approached the question has skewed the debate in an unbiblical way, focusing on overarching paradigms rather than individual points of biblical application.

In part 3 of this book, to address the same theme differently, we will

---

[9] For Niebuhr's discussion, Ibid., 29–39. This quote is from D. A. Carson, *Christ and Culture Revisited* (Grand Rapids; Cambridge: Eerdmans, 2008), 12.

[10] Quoted from my paper, *To Love God with All One's Heart, Soul, and Strength: A Christian Philosophy of Education*, 5-6. Available at Teleioteti.ca/papers. In that paper, the following are cited as sources for this definition: John M. Frame, *The Doctrine of the Christian Life*, A Theology of Lordship 4 (Phillipsburg: P&R Publishing, 2008), 854–857; Henry R. Van Til, *The Calvinistic Concept of Culture* (Grand Rapids: Baker Book House, 1959), 27–33; Carson, *Christ and Culture Revisited*, 67–70.

[11] Timothy Keller, *Center Church: Doing Balanced, Gospel-Centered Ministry in Your City* (Grand Rapids: Zondervan, 2012).

consider how the doctrines of ecclesiology, soteriology, and eschatology shape the way individual Christians and churches conduct themselves in this culture and any culture in which they sojourn. I hope to offer a constructive view of Christian practice within the world, a view that simultaneously sees every culture as home, a place Christians can love and where they can faithfully live for Christ in exile—awaiting his return—and also as a stronghold of enemy territory that needs to be invaded for the sake of Christ. Discussing the Greek philosophers (particularly the Stoics), G.K. Chesterton observed that for all their ethical discourse, they simply did not love the world enough to do what was necessary to change it. They did not love it enough to give everything to change it, nor did they hate it enough to do what was necessary to see it change. Put simply, "They did not love the city enough to set fire to it."[12] As Christians, we are those called by God to live in the world and find pleasure in the myriad of ways he has designed it to be pleasurable—in food, art, nature, friendship, marriage, sex, and a thousand other things. Yet we are also called to recognise it for what it is, a dying world—the old creation—decaying under the curse and a kingdom of its self-proclaimed god, Satan. We must love it enough to care and hate it enough to do what must be done to change it. This dynamic will be taken up in Part 3. The author of *the Epistle to Diognetus*, a 2nd-century Christian defence of the faith, captures the exilic nature of the Christian life well when he writes,

> [Christians] live in their own homelands but as aliens: they participate in everything as citizens but endure all things as strangers. Every foreign land is their homeland, and every homeland is foreign.[13]

Capturing a different sense of this dynamic, G.K. Chesterton writes in *Orthodoxy*,

> We have to feel the universe at once as an ogre's castle, to be stormed, and yet as our own cottage, to which we can return at

---

[12] G. K. Chesterton, *Orthodoxy*, Kindle. (London: William Clowes and Sons LTD, n.d.), 69.

[13] My translation

evening.[14]

I am writing for pastors, Christians, students—maybe even scholars—who want a reminder of what it means to live as exiles in a hostile world, loving God and neighbour for the glory of Christ until he returns. As in other books I have written, I will continue to use footnotes (more common in scholarly literature than popular-level books) to point the reader to relevant literature and to provide explanatory notes; these will be unnecessary for some readers but may prove helpful to others. The selective bibliography provided at the end will give the reader an idea of who has influenced this book and whom they can read for a different opinion or further reading.

As indicated above, I have adopted a three-fold structure for the book. In Part 1, we will consider how Christianity has interacted with Western Culture in the past. This will be important to understand the perspectives many Evangelicals take towards culture in our day, especially Western culture, and my own perspective on their present interaction. The argument of Part 1 will be that Christianity ought not to be identified with Western Culture and that much we Christians identify as truly good about the West is Christian, not Western.

Part 2 will address the perspectives taken by contemporary Evangelicals towards Western culture. It will be shown that many Evangelicals implicitly or explicitly see Western culture as the best conduit for the Gospel and God's purposes, or as the best culture we have, and so ought to be preserved within the Church and in our culture at large. I will argue that this approach is misguided.

Part 3 will bring together the observations and argument of Part 1 & 2 to provide several suggestions on how ecclesiology, soteriology, and eschatology can guide our decision making as individuals and churches. Drawing on the evocative language of Chesterton, I will argue that the Christian approach to the Western world—to the whole world—cannot be to preserve or maintain it. Instead, we must love the Western world—indeed, the whole world—enough to watch it burn. We cannot be those of whom it is charged, "they did not love the [world] enough to set fire to it." We are insurgents, citizens of a different kingdom and servants of a different king,

---

[14] Chesterton, *Orthodoxy*, 64.

but we love this city. We once called it home. Now we recognise the good for which God intended it, especially the people within it. We live within it to see it burn, to see the system of corruption and idolatry fall to the ground, in order that its potential might be realised. We live within it in order that Christ's people within it may be saved and a New Creation might be built upon its ruins. Maybe it is by loving the world so passionately that we are willing to burn it to the ground that we may just "[hasten] the coming of the day of God, because of which the heavens will be set on fire and dissolved, and the heavenly bodies will melt as they burn!" (2 Pet 3:12.) For "according to his promise we are waiting for new heavens and a new earth in which righteousness dwells" (2 Pet 3:13).

Before we begin, join me in prayer:

Father in heaven,
    hallowed be your name.
Your kingdom come, your will be done
    on earth, as it is in heaven.
Open our eyes to perceive the work you are doing;
    give us willing hands to participate in this work.
Open our ears to hear your word clearly;
    give us the hearts to respond as you will.
Amen.

PART 1—

Did Christianity Save the West?

1

WESTERN CULTURE

> ²¹ For although they knew God, they did not honor him as God or give thanks to him, but they became futile in their thinking, and their foolish hearts were darkened. ²² Claiming to be wise, they became fools, ²³ and exchanged the glory of the immortal God for images resembling mortal man and birds and animals and creeping things. – Romans 1:21-23

Western culture is not the oldest culture in the world, nor was it particularly pervasive before the reign of Alexander the Great Hellenised the ancient world or the Roman Empire expanded across three continents. However, it has endured for over 2500 years, and its influence is felt across the globe, even in cultures that explicitly repudiate it. Not only has the technology produced under the auspices of Western civilisation spread across the globe, but its philosophies have shaped civilisations as foreign as China and cultures as alien as Islam.[1] Western civilisation as we know it has many different influences—especially in its Postmodern form—but what is often identified as "Western Culture" today can be divided into at least two streams. First, there is Greco-Roman culture that existed before Christ and has evolved since then. Second, there is the influence of Christianity alongside and in tension with this stream. All I want to do in this and the following two chapters is show that much of what we collapse into our concept of "Western

---

[1] The impact of communism on China is obvious, but the influence of Aristotelian philosophy on Islamic theology may be less so.

Culture" is distinctly Christian, not "Western."² Further, I want to identify continuity between traditional, or Greco-Roman, culture and those aspects of our culture today that Christians lament. The point is simple, much that we value about "The West" is properly Christianity, and these values are clearly seen to be what they are, good things, when juxtaposed with the traditional West. The scope of this book and my scholarly limitations mean that this will only be a cursory treatment. That is, there is much about the ancient world that continues today and which Christians find distinctly valuable, but we will not consider these things.

A. Truth and Wisdom

Philosophy as we know it in the West found its birth around the Mediterranean Sea. In Greece, the Ionian and Eleatic schools began to think about the ultimate nature of the world. Abroad, the Pythagoreans thought through questions of human existence and mathematics. Generally speaking, philosophy was birthed in an attempt to move beyond experience and religion to universal and certain knowledge. Philosophy means, etymologically, the love of wisdom. Wisdom for the philosophers is not the biblical idea of right understanding and skill for living before God in the world; instead, it is something like supra-sensual, universal knowledge possessed by those who seek it out not the ordinary man. Of this wisdom, Aristotle writes,

> We suppose first, then, that the wise man knows all things, as far as possible, although he has not knowledge of each of them in detail; secondly, that he who can learn things that are difficult, and not easy for man to know, is wise (sense-perception is common to all, and therefore easy and no mark of Wisdom); again, he who is more exact and more capable of teaching the causes is wiser, in every branch of knowledge; and of the sciences, also, that which is desirable on its own account and for the sake of knowing it is more

---

[2] This thesis has received confirmation from Tom Holland's recent book. Holland, who is to the best of my knowledge not a Christian, argues that Christianity not Greco-Roman culture is responsible for Western values and its ethic at its best. Tom Holland, *Dominion: How the Christian Revolution Remade the World*, First US edition. (New York: Basic Books, 2019).

of the nature of Wisdom than that which is desirable on account of its results, and the superior science is more of the nature of Wisdom than the ancillary; for the wise man must not be ordered but must order, and he must not obey another, but the less wise must obey him.[3]

The Greek philosophers tried to go as far as reason would take them towards universal knowledge of everything. For some, like Aristotle, this included considerations of what right living ought to look like. For others, like Plato, this meant looking for goodness itself instead of what acts are good and ought to be done. However, for both Aristotle and Plato, and those who descended from them, their concern was the unity or unchanging reality behind the flux of the experienced world. Instead of considering trees and the beauty of the stars, they sought to understand what made a tree a tree (that element all trees had in common) and the causes for change and movement in the world. This mode of Philosophy did not produce what we recognise as good in Western culture; indeed, it often produced what we lament as the death of Western culture.

The worst of Modern philosophies have produced atheism, tyranny, ethical relativism, and (in my opinion) much wasted time. Greek philosophy produced much the same. In his Republic, Plato argues in a manner similar to Aristotle as quoted above. Plato argues that because philosophers are those with wisdom, they ought to bear the burden of rule.[4] His picture of a philosopher led aristocracy and dominion is closer to the tyranny of the privileged and powerful than modern democracy. "Atheism" is not an easy term to peg down in the ancient world (it was sometimes thrown at Christians for rejecting the Roman pantheon), yet it can apply in many ways to the Philosophers of the ancient world. For one, philosophy itself as it was birthed

---

[3] Aristotle, "Metaphysics," in *The Works of Aristotle*, ed. W. D. Rose and J. A. Smith, Logos Edition., vol. 8 (Oxford: The Clarendon Press, 1908), bks. 1, Ch. 2.

[4] "'Unless,' said I, 'either philosophers become kings in our states or those whom we now call our kings and rulers take to the pursuit of philosophy seriously and adequately, and there is a conjunction of these two things, political power and philosophic intelligence, while the motley horde of the natures who at present pursue either apart from the other are compulsorily excluded, there can be no cessation of troubles, dear Glaucon, for our states, nor, I fancy, for the human race either.'" Plato, *The Republic: English Text*, ed. T. E. Page et al. (Cambridge, MA; London: Harvard University Press; William Heinemann Ltd., 1937), 5.473c-d.

in the Greek world was a repudiation of the Greek religion and its explanations for reality. In its place, Aristotle created a god of reason, an unmoved mover: this "god" does not interact directly with the world and has no content. This "god" is merely thought thinking thought. Aristotle's "god" exists as the goal of all change and so is responsible for all the natural order yet does not and cannot act or be acted upon. In this way, Aristotle's god is much like the god of Enlightenment deism. Plato uses the term "god" (θεός), yet it is unclear what exactly is god in his system. God, for Plato, does not speak and make himself known in the world. Potentially, god is an impersonal perfection that is the ultimate object of thought and action but cannot act or govern humanity in any meaningful way. For Democritus and the atomists, the explanation of all things was chance, the purely contingent interaction of the smallest, indivisible objects, "atoms." In these ways, like modern atheism and secularism, humanity was left on its own; God had not spoken authoritatively, so there was no absolute reference point for meaning. The Socratic method of dialectic explored the meaning and parameters of language but was unable to arrive at definite conclusions, easily leading to scepticism. These philosophers, and the stoics after them, spent much time identifying ethical norms and seeking to identify the virtuous life, but this was not the only and maybe not even the most influential movement in Greek and, later, Roman culture. There were also the Sophists, the relativists, who did not systemise and reason towards abstract truth but who made a living teaching rhetoric and who lived by a pragmatist ethic—namely, what was good and right was what worked, made a living, and created order in society.

The 20th-century philosopher and mathematician Alfred North Whitehead once said that all of Western Philosophy consisted of "a series of footnotes to Plato."[5] Considering the heritage bequeathed to us by the Greek philosophers, this is not saying much. The result has been consistently naturalism, scepticism, and futility. We have not got closer to understanding God, his word, or his world. The influence of Western Philosophy on contemporary society is pervasive, yet looking beneath the surface, this

---

[5] Alfred North Whitehead, *Process and Reality*, (Simon and Schuster, 2010), 39.

heritage is not often a good thing.[6]

B. Freedom and Equality

Shifting gears for a second, some of the most valued aspects of Western society are Freedom and (the pursuit of) equality. As I write this, many have protested what they have interpreted as heavy-handed government action to handle the COVID-19 pandemic, and 20th and 21st century have experienced continued efforts through violent and non-violent protests, lobbying, and legislation to bring about equality between races and genders. At least on the popular account, these are characteristics inherited from Pre-Christian Western culture. Is not democracy an invention of the ancient world? Is it not the pinnacle of Western civilisation? Assuming for the sake of argument that this is true, "democracy" does not necessarily equal freedom or equality. Sure, it beats Communism and many other forms of tyranny, but a tyranny of the masses is surely not better than a tyranny of the one. If humanity is as bad as the Bible teaches us, then what we can expect from democracy is what we see today; sexual license, legalised murder (euthanasia, abortion), etc. In the Bible, true justice, true freedom, true equality is established by the rule of a perfect and righteous king. I long to live in a world ruled by a truly righteous, just king! We have seen in recent experience what we find early in the book of Samuel: when the people choose their king, the result is tragedy (cf. 1 Samuel 8 – 2 Samuel 1).

However, only some of what we know today as democracy is rooted in the ancient world. The Greeks had civic elections and representative democracy, yet this did not stop frequent wars and moral perversion from taking hold in that peninsula. The Roman Republic was a non-democratic oligarchy, ruled by a small number of powerful families. What we prize most about Western polity—freedom—is by no means rooted in these early civilisations. There is much continuity to be sure, yet there was an insufficient objective or transcendent ground for the limited freedoms granted by Greek democracy, for example. In a time of war or in a couple of generations, it

---

[6] I argue this in my books *The Gift of Knowing* (Vancouver, Teleioteti 2019), *The Gift of Seeing* (Vancouver, Teleioteti forthcoming), and—to a limited extent—my PhD Thesis (in progress).

could become a part of the great kingdom of Alexander, an oligarchy, or a part of the Roman Republic, which itself became subject to tyranny. In the ancient world, as Hegel put it, "one was free" or "some were free," but it was not until the modern world that "all are free."[7] Indeed, the rich and powerful may have had some forms of freedom—even a voice in the decisions of the culture—yet slavery was rampant and accepted. Now, this was not the slavery of ancient Egypt or the American South, yet it was brutal nonetheless. It took something foreign to Greco-Roman society to introduce anything like Hegel's ideal of "all are free," and even then, this has often only existed in idea, not reality. A foundation for equality of men and women, slave and free, black and white, unborn and elderly, is not found in traditional Western culture but in the Bible. All people *ought* to be free and *ought* to be treated equally because all have been made in the image of God. All people are created to represent him and equipped to do so. In Christ, the universal declaration of judgment and the universal availability of salvation along with citizenship provides the unequivocal foundation for freedom and equality, where there is neither slave nor free, Jew nor Greek, man nor woman, but all are one in Christ (Gal 3:28). Apart from an authoritative declaration to this effect, there is no transcendent foundation or good reason to insist that all *ought* to be free or equal. This is why biblical equality is not what we have witnessed in ancient and modern Western societies.

From a Christian vantage point, we would rightly be appalled at much that characterised the ancient West, as much as we are by what characterises the contemporary West. For example, like the West as late as the 20th century, only men were able to vote in the Greek democracies. In addition to slavery, some of our worst ethical issues were rampant in this ancient world.

C. Mercy and Humility

---

[7] We can of course debate how true that is of our present age, or the age of Modernism when Hegel wrote this. However, if Western culture is to be praised for the ideal of freedom, this does not find its root in the ancient Greco-Roman world. Hegel interpreted history from the vantage point of 18th and 19th century Prussia (modern Germany) as the progressive evolution of the idea of freedom in human civilization. Civilization gradually progressive from slavery to nature (none are free) to tyranny, oligarchy, and finally modern Western political and societal "freedom."

Most significantly, the virtues of mercy and humility were unknown, even decried as weakness, in the ancient West. It was not a virtue to refuse glory and honour, to point to God as the giver of all good things instead of the self. And what value was there in helping those who were weak? The opposite of mercy may be cold indifference, common in fatalistic societies (of which the ancient Greco-Roman religions and culture were an example), or it may be to delight in the suffering of others. Crucifixion may have predated the Romans, but they surely perfected and widely exploited its horrific potential. Roman society was famously the home of gladiatorial combat. Here, slaughter and gore served as entertainment for the people (which does not sound too far from our current cultural climate). Sexual exploitation was pervasive and accepted, included pederasty. Homosexuality was common, and many religious rituals involved illicit sexual activity. For all the ethical discussions among the philosophers, their ideals did not shape the general ethical ethos of the populous—at least not in the direction of God's moral order.

Maybe I am painting a one-sided picture, you may be thinking, yet there is a reason for this. If we take seriously Paul's claim that all men and women know God yet reject him and exchange him along with his standard of goodness and truth for idolatry, we can and should expect pervasive idolatry and ethical bankruptcy in human culture. The fact that we find good at all in any society, including the ancient West, is an example of his generous kindness and goodness—providing rain and sunshine to the good and evil alike (Matt 5:45). The point I am making is this: if we are going idolise an ancient culture and its heritage, let's be frank about it. We cannot just pick and choose what we would like. The ancient West may have contributed many things that we find good and true today, yet it has also produced a lasting heritage of idolatry and immorality. Its artwork, plays, and poems reflect the social values and worldview that led to all of its faults. That must be kept in mind even if we may find aesthetic, historical, or pedagogical value in its heritage.

2

BIBLICALLY INFLUENCED CULTURE

Western Culture as we know it today has received an inheritance from ancient Western culture, but it has also received a uniquely Christian inheritance. The same vices, problems, and social dynamics that plagued the ancient world have remained in its children, the Roman Empire, Christianised Europe, and Modern world. However, somethings did change—many things changed—as the Gospel permeated Western civilisation. Something must have happened for much slavery to end, for mercy to become laudable, and for the lethal injection to replace crucifixion (i.e. for a relatively peaceful death penalty to replace a torturous one). What changed was not the progressive evolution of human reason or a human invention. What happened was the spread of the Gospel throughout the Western world: individual Christians and their churches living in ways that challenged and overthrew the social norms of the ancient world. I do not wish to put forth what follows as a commendation or recommendation for Christian action, as if we only need to do this, then we will see a Christian empire! Instead, I hope to illustrate that Christianity is something uniquely different than Western culture, and it shines forth against the background of the ancient world.[1] The point is this, if we want to see society change in a positive direction (whether that should be our goal or not is of course in question)—if we want to see our children live in a Christ-like manner (that at least must be our goal)—*ressourcing* and returning to the ancient world is not the answer. *Ressourcing* and returning

---

[1] See further, Rodney Stark, *The Rise of Christianity: A Sociologist Reconsiders History* (Princeton University Press, 1996); Holland, *Dominion*.

to the Word of God that shown forth so gloriously is the answer.

A. The Distinct Lives of Early Christians

Christians did not stand out against Western Culture or even achieve lasting change in it by an intentional social-political agenda or by lobby efforts. Change happened, a difference was seen, when men and women lived lives that were distinctly different—drastically different than their neighbours. This led to the rapid growth of Christianity and a change in the behaviour of Christians and even their neighbours. In a letter commending the faith to one Diognetus, an anonymous early Christian described the distinctive life of early Christians in this manner:

> For the distinction between Christians and other men, is neither in country nor language nor customs. For they do not dwell in cities in some place of their own, nor do they use any strange variety of dialect, nor practise an extraordinary kind of life. This teaching of theirs has not been discovered by the intellect or thought of busy men, nor are they the advocates of any human doctrine as some men are. Yet while living in Greek and barbarian cities, according as each obtained his lot, and following the local customs, both in clothing and food and in the rest of life, they show forth the wonderful and confessedly strange character of the constitution of their own citizenship. They dwell in their own fatherlands, but as if sojourners in them; they share all things as citizens, and suffer all things as strangers. Every foreign country is their fatherland, and every fatherland is a foreign country. They marry as all men, they bear children, but they do not expose their offspring. They offer free hospitality, but guard their purity. Their lot is cast "in the flesh," but they do not live "after the flesh." They pass their time upon the earth, but they have their citizenship in heaven. They obey the appointed laws, and they surpass the laws in their own lives. They love all men and are persecuted by all men. They are unknown and they are condemned. They are put to death and they gain life. "They are poor and make many rich" they lack all things and have all things in abundance. [14]They are dishonoured, and are glorified in their dishonour, they are spoken evil of and are justified. "They are abused and give blessing," they are insulted and render honour. When they do good they are buffeted as evil-doers,

when they are buffeted they rejoice as men who receive life. They are warred upon by the Jews as foreigners and are persecuted by the Greeks, and those who hate them cannot state the cause of their enmity.[2]

Sociologist Rodney Stark has documented the way Christians interacted with the Roman world and how their behaviour transformed that world in his book *The Rise of Christianity*. He argues that Constantine's edict of Milan did not grant Christianity cultural ascendency but was rather a response to "rapid Christian growth that had already made them a major political force."[3] He documents in that book many different ways the alternate lives of Christians led to such a transformation. Christians grew up steeped in the Roman culture, but their conversion to Christ led them to abandon many values and customs and take up drastically different ones in submission to Christ's lordship. Believing that every human being, no matter their age or sex, bore the image of God, Christians renounced all practices of abortion and infanticide.[4] Instead of joining in the Roman culture of death, they renounced these practices as murderous and forewent participation in the events that revelled in death.[5] Christian attitudes towards women and marriage stood in stark contrast with the misogynistic behaviour of the Romans, and the value Christians placed on marriage and sexual purity contrasted vividly with the disdain for marriage and sexual fidelity held by many Romans.[6] Because they valued love, charity, and the sanctity of human life, Christians showed great courage in risking their lives to take care of both their fellow Christians and even pagans during the great epidemics that devastated the population of the Roman Empire during the first few centuries AD. They nursed the sick and treated even the dead with respect, sometimes losing their lives in the process.[7] This behaviour was vastly

---

[2] *The Epistle to Diognetus*, sec. V in Kirsopp Lake, trans., *The Apostolic Fathers* (Cambridge MA; London: Harvard University Press, 1912).

[3] Rodney Stark, *The Rise of Christianity: A Sociologist Reconsiders history* (Princeton University Press, 1996), 2.Stark, 2

[4] Ibid., 124–125.

[5] Ibid., 214–215.

[6] Ibid., 104, 117, 123.

[7] Ibid., 73, 82–83, 87.

different from that of the Romans, who fled the cities, left the sick to die, and treated the bodies of the dead as dirt.[8] Through lives transformed by the Gospel, Christianity injected something new into pagan Greco-Roman culture.

B. The Christianised world

Many of the most significantly "Western" institutions are those that came about because of this Gospel injections. Education as we know it came about at the end of a long effort by Christians to introduce literacy and skill training throughout the world. Hospitals as we know them today had their origins in Christian care ministry.[9] Hegel was wrong about many things, but he did witness in Europe a sort of freedom unparalleled in the ancient world (at least the non-God-fearing ancient world). This freedom has never been realised fully, yet the biblical teaching of the image of God put all humanity on a level playing field. Man or woman, slave or free, Jew or Gentile, king or servant, every human is made by God, accountable to God, and given purpose by God. Many of the freedoms we treasure in Western society result from biblical principles or explicit theology. As some argued for the divine right of the king, others like Samuel Rutherford argued that God's law was higher than the king.[10] Values such as mercy, compassion, care for the orphan and downtrodden are distinctly Christian virtues; even when appropriated in a non-Christian form, the impetus for such values comes from a biblical worldview.

The point I want to make is a simple one: many of the features of "the West" that contemporary writers want to retrieve are not found by going back to the Greeks, to a Christian-Greek synthesis, or the Enlightenment.

---

[8] Ibid., 83, 85–86.

[9] As a modern example, the Christian mission to Korea in the late 19th century and early 20th century often centred around establishing hospitals. Cf. J. Alexander Rutherford, "Faith Comes through Hearing, and Hearing through the Word of Christ: The Centrality of Scripture in the Early Presbyterian Missions to Korea (1884-1910)" (Teleioteti, 2017).

[10] Samuel Rutherford, *Lex, Rex, or the Law and the Prince* (Edinburgh: R. Ogle, 1843).

They are found by going back to the Holy Scriptures. Even Science, often used as a tool against the claims of the Bible, is arguably a Christian invention.

C. The Christian Foundation of Sciences

Why is it that the hard sciences as we know them only emerged in recent history? Many factors can be traced, but many authors today argue that the hard sciences emerged only because of the Renaissance and Reformation emphasis on going back to Scripture. In favour of this, some might point to the Christian faith or worldview of the early pioneers of the sciences. However, Christians were at the pinnacle of thought for the preceding 1000 years, but the hard sciences did not emerge. Something changed in the very pursuit of knowledge. One factor may be developments in logic during the Dark Ages that turned the focus of knowledge from abstract truths to the concrete objects of experience. One 20th century author argued something like this, though he looked at the influence of Reformation biblicism.[11] He asked the question, what caused the change from Aristotle to Bacon? Aristotle, like the scientists, was interested in the realm of experience, yet he could care less about the actual experience of an object. For him, true knowledge, or wisdom, was not the basic experience all humans share; it was something else. This knowledge depended on experience but was not experience. He argued that something is truly and fully known if you know its causes (he identified four causes). The problem was, in each case, the causes of one particular was also the cause of all things in its class (a pot is specific matter formed according to the pattern of a pot by a craftsman for a specific end shared by all pots). The knowledge worth having is knowledge of everything, not specific things (see the quote from Aristotle above on the nature of philosophy); the very features that differentiate one pot from another, its matter and accidents (features that do not factor into its being a pot, colour, size, location, etc.), are incidental to knowledge.

---

[11] M. B. Foster, "The Christian Doctrine of Creation and the Rise of Modern Natural Science," *Mind* 43, no. 172 (1934): 446–468; M.B. Foster, "Christian Theology and Modern Science of Nature (Part 1)," *Mind* 44 (1935): 439–466; M.B. Foster, "Christian Theology and Modern Science of Nature (Part 2)," *Mind* 45 (1936): 1–27.

Science, on the other hand, cares about details: it is the individuality of objects that point to universal laws governing their interactions, and it is individual things that can put to use. It is a subtle difference—and I argue elsewhere that science has not escaped Aristotle—but it is a real difference. Foster argued that the difference came about because of the Christian doctrine of creation.[12] If God created individual things, if God acts in history in particular ways, then maybe the individual things science investigates, the individual objects of experience, are valuable. Whether Foster is correct or not, something changed to bring about the natural sciences. Good arguments can be made Christianity supplied the personal beliefs and overarching worldview that allowed the sciences to emerge. My point is this: the sciences we value and technology its products, are not rooted in pre-Christian Western culture. These things emerged from a culture saturated in the biblical worldview—even when rebelling against it. Christianity has offered something distinctly good and new in contrast with this heritage. We cannot confuse the two. Christianity shone forth against the backdrop of the West because it was distinct from it; today, as the West becomes more like its ancient predecessors and less like the biblical ideals, this distinction will become more and more clear, which can only do good for our Christian witness.

---

[12] Foster, "The Christian Doctrine of Creation and the Rise of Modern Natural Science." More recently, Johannes Zachhuber has argued that Christian theologians initiated a transformation in philosophy as they wrestled through the implications of Chalcedonian Christology, particularly their philosophy shifted the focus from unity and to particularity or the individual. This latter emphasis is that which Foster finds in the doctrine of Creation. My PhD thesis identifies this same change in the 4th and 5th centuries, as Christians began to wrestle with the incarnation in light of Nicene Trinitarianism. Johannes Zachhuber, *The Rise of Christian Theology and the End of Ancient Metaphysics: Patristic Philosophy from the Cappadocian Fathers to John of Damascus* (Oxford University Press, 2020).

3

DID CHRISTIANITY SAVE THE WEST?

Christianity has contributed a lot of good to Western culture over the years. However, Christianity is still widespread in the Western world, yet that world is fragmenting in a myriad of ways. Though this view is rightly rejected today, it used to be said that the with the sacking of Rome, the "West" collapsed, and the "Dark Ages" began. Some Romans apparently saw it this way. When the West supposedly fell, when Rome was sacked by the "Barbarian" hordes, the pagans blamed Christianity. "You led us to forsake our gods," they screamed, "you let our sacrificial fires burn out! This is their vengeance, and you are at fault!" Saint Augustine countered this with a doctrine of history. "Get your facts straight," he argued. The empire has prospered and endured these last 400 years with a Christian influence—nearly a century with Christian emperors. "But do not be confused," he argued, "there is a greater conflict here; Rome is just a piece of the puzzle." Man constructs its empires, yet it is God's city—his people—that will endure through the ages. Rome may have fallen, but what made it the greatest continues throughout history.[1] The pagan critics overstated their case, and Augustine's sweeping interpretation of history may not have been perfect, but the idea the West was lost and then restored by Christianity remains popular today. As with many things in history, however, it is a lot more complicated than that.

---

[1] Saint Augustine, *Saint Augustine: The City of God*, trans. Gerald G. Walsh and Mother Grace Monahan, vol. 7, The Fathers of the Church: The Writings of Augustine 14 (Washington, D.C.: The Catholic University of America Press, Inc., 1981).

Not only Christianity but Western culture continued after the sacking of Rome. What followed was actually a period of new order, philosophical and artistic development, and the emergence of a more thoroughgoing Christian empire in the West, under Charlemagne. In the East, the Eastern Roman or Byzantine empire continued and flourished. "The Dark Ages" proved to be not so dark after all. Greek philosophy was prominent. In the West, the focus was mostly on Aristotle's logic, not the greater worldview he and the rest of the Greek philosophers espoused.

It is in this time, with the flourishing of the West, East, and Islam that the Renaissance happened, what some see as the saving of the West. After Rome and the Western Roman Empire fell, it might seem as though a thousand years of Greco-Roman culture was lost. Non-withstanding that the "Barbarian" invaders were steeped in this tradition as well, there was still the Eastern Empire. In fact, the Eastern Empire, with its capital in Constantinople, would remain for hundreds of years as a flourishing centre of Greek language and tradition. Indeed, in monastic communities, many ancient works were copied and kept for future generations. Then came Islam. When Islam sacked Constantinople, and the Eastern Empire fell, the monks and others came running to their Western Christian brothers with a living Greek language and copies of the original languages of the Bible and Greek culture.[2] So began the Renaissance.

A. The Renaissance

The Renaissance saw a resurgence in the arts and the classics, a retrieval of Aristotelian metaphysics, and revival in the Church. However, the Renaissance did not see a dead West reborn; instead, it saw the meeting of different Western traditions.

Protestantism was born, and the road to the Enlightenment was paved. With a resurgence in the pre-Christian West came a resurgence of the Pre-

---

[2] History is always too complicated to be packaged up so simply. For example, not only did Greek scholars and monks bring Greek works to the West, but Islamic scholars discovered Aristotle and contributed to the interpretation of Aristotle and others in the West.

Christian problems. Atheism and deism began to grow, and in the intelligentsia, the moral corruption of the Pre-Christian West began to emerge. With the loss of Roman Catholic pre-eminence, there was an authority vacuum. This hole was filled with the self. Rene Descartes famously undertook the project of building all human knowledge on the foundation of the immediate certainty of one's own existence: *cogito ergo sum*, "I think therefore I am." In many ways, this claim was in strong continuity with the ancient West: though Platonism had identified the ground for knowledge in a transcendent reality, the only access humanity had to this reality was in their own minds. Though Plato, Aristotle, and their heirs may have rejected Protagoras' claim that man was the measure of all things, the doctrine of forms and Aristotle's logic both came down to what humanity had access to within themselves. However, the newness of Christianity did not disappear; Descartes himself at least claimed to be a Christian. The Modern West lived on borrowed capital, often rejecting God and the Bible on the one hand while presupposing his faithfulness on the other, having blind faith in the orderliness and intelligibility of the world.

With Hume came a significant blow to this heritage: he argued that we cannot know anything with certainty and have only blind belief at the foundation of what we can know. Hume woke Kant "from his dogmatic slumber," but Kant was able to save human knowledge and the sciences by bifurcating the world: we cannot know the world out there, beyond our minds, but we can understand the world created by the rational faculties of our mind. Scepticism thus became enshrined in philosophy: we cannot know the world as it may or may not exist outside our minds. This scepticism would catch up with the sciences in the 20th century. Then came nihilism, the practical outworking of atheism. As Nietzsche provocatively illustrated, the West had killed god but was unwilling to face the consequences. When they finally owned up to the new reality, purposelessness, hopelessness, and no absolute reality would confront them:

> "What were we doing when we unchained this earth from its sun?" spoke the madman, "Where is it moving to now? Where are we moving to? Away from all suns? Are we not continually falling? And backwards, sidewards, forwards, in all directions? Is there still an up and a down? Aren't we straying as though through an infinite

nothing?"³

The 20th century and the 21st century have simply worked out what was already present in the Hellenistic philosophy as well as the Enlightenment and Modernism: without a transcendent God and his revelation, morality and knowledge are measured by the mind of humanity, whether its cultures or individuals. The West today looks awfully like the ancient West.⁴

B. In Sum, It's Complicated

So, what can be said about the West and Christianity? Did Christianity save the west? Is the West worth saving? Our answer can only be, "it's complicated." In one sense, we have to answer no: the West was never lost, so it did not need to be saved. However, Christianity has had a lasting contribution that has led to flourishing in the Western world.

In another sense, Christianity has contributed to our contemporary crisis. By preserving Greco-Roman tradition, Christianity has preserved the atheistic rationalism and deism that characterised the ancient world. By undermining the authority of the Catholic church, the Protestant Reformation may have hastened the fragmentation of our society, into individuals and group identities without unity. Consider several more examples. By excommunicating the Arians and claiming Nicaean Christianity as its own, Rome was set against the Arians that would be its downfall. Without Christianity, the Arab tribes would never have been unified in Islam, what some consider to be a Christian heresy. Islam has often been perceived as the biggest threat to the European West over the last millennium. Secularism and much of "the Left"—whatever we may mean by that

---

³ This is taken from Kaufmann's translation of *The Gay Science*. Friedrich Wilhelm Nietzsche and Walter Kaufmann, *Basic Writings of Nietzsche*, Modern Library ed. (New York: Modern Library, 2000).

⁴ I argue for the continuity between Hellenistic, Modern, and Postmodern philosophy in the first part of this series (God's Gifts for the Christian Life – Part 1). Especially in J. Alexander Rutherford, *The Gift of Knowing: A biblical Perspective on Knowing and Truth*, God's Gifts for the Christian Life Part 1 Vol. 1 (Vancouver: Teleioteti, 2019).

moniker—has built itself on its opposition to Christianity. Secularism is technically the exclusion of religion from the public sphere, but this animus is often focused on Christianity and maybe Islam. Marxism appropriates the postmillennial view of history's progress and sets itself against all religion, often explicitly against Christianity.

So much of what we treasure in the West is the result of the Gospel, but Christianity has in its own way drawn out what we despise most. Perhaps Christianity staved of the inevitable collapse of the West under the weight of its contradictions. However, Christianity—or what passes as Christianity—is often now the antagonist driving the West's self-destruction. Christians act to restrain evil, and their opponents double down on that same evil. People disown Christianity only to welcome Islam as a replacement for the meaning they lost in the process. Secularism is killing the West, and Christianity provoked it. Science and philosophy are killing the West, and Christianity nurtured and preserved them. Many claim Islam is killing the West, but it is welcomed as the alternative to Christianity. Did Christianity save the West? It's complicated.

But what now? Whether or not Christianity saved the West, should it save the West? Many Christians answer "Yes!" to this question. Yet once again, it's complicated. Can we enjoy the great benefits of living in Western society? Of course, these are blessings from God. We have enjoyed unparalleled freedoms and opportunities because of the Christian influence on the West. I would love to have lived only 70 years ago when my daughter would have had a generally safer upbringing. But recognising and thanking God for a good gift does not mean we should fight to retain that gift. For one, the "West," as we have seen, is a mixed bag: good and bad are found side by side in its history. So, we must be clear: saving the West, for a Christian, can only mean treasuring and fighting for the Gospel which has influenced it. Should we do this, seek to restrain the West's demise and attempt to transform it into a more Christ-like empire, a "Mere Christendom"?[5]

---

[5] "Mere Christendom" is the phrase used by Douglas Wilson in his book, *Empires of Dirt*. Douglas Wilson, *Empires of Dirt: Secularism, Radical Islam, and the Mere Christendom Alternative* (Moscow, Ida.: Canon Press, 2016). Cf. Appendix 1.

I want to suggest in the following two parts that this should not be our goal or even our desire. Indeed, I want to argue that we should welcome the West's demise—whether it is tomorrow or in a thousand years—and the rise of whatever beastly empire with which God chooses to replace it. In Part 2, we will consider different ways Christians have answered the question, how should we live in the culture around us? Many of these positions would affirm that the West ought to be saved; we will see why that is not the best answer to this question. However, before we turn there, I want to end this first part with a simple observation that ought to make us question our love for the West.

Whether you are postmillennial, amillennial, or premillennial in your eschatology, I think you can agree with me that the central burden of the Church's mission is to see people who are in rebellion against God and under his wrath transferred into the kingdom of his glorious Son, delivered from wrath and free to enjoy him forever. We need to ask ourselves, where in the Bible—and in history—does this happen most effectively? Has it happened under "Christendom" or outside of it? In the New Testament, Christendom is not present—even as an ideal. Instead, Christianity thrives under persecution. "If the world hates you," Jesus told his disciples, "know that it has hated me before it hated you. If you were of the world, the world would love you as its own; but because you are not of the world, but I chose you out of the world, therefore the world hates you" (John 15:18-19). "Do not be surprised, brothers," writes John, "that the world hates you" (1 John 3:13). However, far from a detriment, this persecution continually led to the Church's growth. As Tertullian is famously misquoted, "the blood of the martyrs is the seed of the church."[6] Indeed, it is in and through persecution that Christianity so prospered in the first three centuries AD that it came to dominate the Western world. However, the situation looked quite different in the 4th and 5th centuries (which I am studying extensively for my PhD). The position of power enjoyed by the church after the conversion of Constantine and the resolution of the Arian controversy did not lead to the spread of the Gospel and Christian faith. Instead, many bishops fought for more power, fought against one another, and excommunicated and killed one

---

[6] The original, *Plures efficimur, quotiens metimur a vobis: semen est sanguis Christianorum.* "We multiply as often as we are reaped by you: the blood of Christians is seed." Tertullian, *The Apology,* ch. 50. My translation.

another for the sake of ecclesiastical and imperial unity.

What would have happened if they were less concerned with whom they could appoint at bishops and how far their authority would extend and, instead, focused on going forth and baptising and teaching pagans and nominal Christians alike to love and worship God according to the Scriptures? Only God knows, but it would probably look different than it does now. Fast forward 1200 years. After the Protestant Reformation, "Christian" Europe began to show its less-than-Christian underbelly. The worldview was there, yes, but faith was not. State churches dried up into a dead orthodoxy or liberal theology, much like the Catholic church before it. Life in the church was not found in steady, faithful teaching and preaching but in periodic awakenings that saw revival for a few generations. These revivals were so distinct because the "Christian" culture around them was anything but Christian; the presence of true faith was set up in striking relief. Even here, the effects of the revivals tapered off after a short while. The 19th and 20th centuries saw many of "mainline," or historic, Protestant denominations in North America descend into unchristian liberalism, a development that was echoed in many other countries. That is, for all its pretence of Christendom, the West has been a miserable place to find vibrant Christian life.

Where we see the Gospel taking hold of people and transforming their lives is not the last bastions of Christendom; it is in the most anti-Christian places. Communist China is quickly becoming the most populous Christian nation, despite its virulent anti-Christian agenda. Islamic Iran, Iraq, Syria, Lebanon, Palestine, and Northern Africa have healthy and growing Christian populations, despite persecution. In the Russian church, there are many signs of life, despite efforts by the Soviet Union to extinguish it. These days, there is much talk about "Global Christianity" because Christianity has a truly global presence. It sometimes appears that the church is thriving everywhere but the West. Do we really want to save the one earthly kingdom where Christians are encouraged to live tepid lives and often do so? A kingdom where so many people do not even bother to ask the questions to which Christianity offers answers? I was struck a while back, reading an article about Christianity in Iran, by the observation of an Iranian couple who moved back to Iran *for the sake of their own faith*; they feared for the health of their faith living in the West.[7]

It may seem morbid and even heartless, but I am encouraged by the direction the West is taking. The farther our society moves from the Bible, the more clearly Christianity will stand out as different and necessary. Christians will also be forced to take a stand: will they follow Jesus or the latest Western idol? Far from a bad thing, I can only see fruit emerging from such a situation. Why? Because historically and biblically, it is in these situations that God people thrive, and people are snatched from the fires of Hell. I wrote an article for The Gospel Coalition Canada to this effect, concluding that secularism may be a blessing for the Church, revealing our need for the Gospel and the answers God has given us in Scripture to a myriad of problems with which our culture is confronted.[8]

We need to love the West—its people, not its institutions—so much that we will watch it burn and suffer the discomfort of a new world if only it means that some are saved and that Christ returns to bring true justice. However, many Christians would disagree on this point, so it is to these alternate positions that we must now turn.

---

[7] I can not track down the reference for this article. It was written by a pastor reflecting on broader Western culture and this couple were acquaintances of his.

[8] James Rutherford, "Benefits of Secularity," *The Gospel Coalition / Canada*, n.d., accessed May 17, 2020, https://ca.thegospelcoalition.org/article/benefits-of-secularity/.

—Part 2—

Should Christianity Save the Western world?

4

STRATEGIES TO SAVE THE WEST

And Jesus came and said to them, "All authority in heaven and on earth has been given to me. Go therefore and make disciples of all nations, baptising them in the name of the Father and of the Son and of the Holy Spirit, teaching them to observe all that I have commanded you. And behold, I am with you always, to the end of the age." – Matthew 28:18-20

All Scripture is breathed out by God and profitable for teaching, for reproof, for correction, and for training in righteousness, that the man of God may be complete, equipped for every good work. – 2 Timothy 3:16-17

"Should Christians save the West?" The answer I have given to this question in the last chapter—that we should not—is not the most common answer given among Reformed and Evangelical circles, but it is not unknown. In the following three chapters, the second part of this book, I want to use "Saving the West" as a lens through which to consider Christian views that see "Culture" in general as a good thing within which Christians have a significant, constructive role. Such positions generally look favourably upon Western culture, some explicitly trying to preserve this culture. In this chapter, I want to consider three strategies employed by some Christians of the Reformed or generally Evangelical persuasion to save the West. Each of these approaches is envisioned as a way Christianity can thrive amidst our present crisis and involves a posture towards the past and future that is positive towards "the West," not just the Gospel but also its broader Greco-Roman heritage.

A. Ressourcement

The first trend or approach to saving the West is Evangelical ressourcement. Ressourcement is a trend within recent theology that looks to the past for answers to present problems. One proponent of ressourcement defines it as "looking to the history of the church for resources to give theological direction to people in the twenty-first century."[1] Though ressourcement could minimally be a return to theological tradition, it often refers to particular intellectual and cultural forms of Christian cultural engagement. Thus, though it does not have to be, it is often a tool for saving the West.

On the fringes of Evangelicalism, there is the Radical Orthodoxy movement. This movement identifies the central problem of secularism as its desacralisation of the universe, collapsing all reality into the sphere of human mental and sensual activity. Our problems began, some argue, with the Reformation and the logical school of nominalism, which is said to have given the seed out of which post-reformation secularisation grew.[2] By emphasising the Bible over tradition and the authority of the individual (it is claimed) over the Church, the Reformation overthrew the Christian-platonic synthesis that had formed the matrix of Christian theology for the last 1500 years. Secularism is the natural result of abandoning this worldview. That is, Radical Orthodoxy claims that the ancient worldview was one where all of our experience, everything in the creation, "participates" in the sacred and so points beyond itself to God (a "sacramental ontology").[3] By rejecting this participation, secularism excludes God out of all life. The answer, for Radical Orthodoxy, is to retrieve this ancient synthesis. To save our society and the Church's ability to speak to its issues, we need to *ressource* the Western

---

[1] Boersma, *Heavenly Participation*, 9.

[2] That is, nominalist rejected the "universals," transcendent realities that gave meaning to our experience. By doing so, Radical Orthodoxy believes they cut God out from everyday life and paved the way for the full exclusion of God.

[3] If your confused about what this means, you have joined many others. Sacramental ontology is not explained clearly in many books and the only person who ever gave a sufficient account of "participation," Plotinus, did so in a way that excludes Christianity. See my paper, "Sacramental Ontology and Augustine's Platonism," www.teleioteti.ca/papers.

philosophical heritage.

With their stance opposing the Reformation and with a generally low view of Scripture, Radical Orthodoxy is not popular among conservatives or the traditionally Reformed, but these groups have their own ressourcement trends. Presbyterians generally have a high view of the Reformers, Reformed creeds, and early church, so it is no surprise that they would turn to these sources for theological perspectives on our culture. However, there is a trend to go back to these sources, even before the Reformation, for answers to the cultural problems of our time, specifically secularism and its effects. Crossway Books has recently been publishing a series to this very end, an effort to ressource "The Christian Intellectual Tradition." In areas such as philosophy, education, and politics, this series intends to present historical, Western answers to contemporary Western problems.

What ought we make of this effort? Is it a viable tool or model for Christian interaction with contemporary culture? I want to register a resounding "No!" to that question. I think this effort overvalues tradition—especially Western tradition—and undervalues Scripture. After exploring these two issues, I want to consider one specific ressourcement project undertaken by Reformed Evangelicals.

First, the ressourcement project, in general, overvalues tradition. Many of these ressourcement projects treat the philosophical and practical teachings of the Church as sources for Christian theology of and interaction with culture. The questions we need to ask ourselves are, what reason do we have for believing the Fathers had better philosophies of culture than we do? By what authority do we measure such superiority? To put it in other words, why should we believe that pre-Modern culture is better than Modern or Postmodern culture? There is, apart from Scripture, no way to do so. Though it is true that newer is not always better, it is equally true that older is not always better. In many demonstrable ways, Modern and Postmodern culture has helped us to better understand God, his world, and our mission. If we use Scripture as our guide, we find that Premodern culture is as problematic as Modern and Postmodern culture. Furthermore, if we are going back to Scripture as our standard, we really are not ressourcing anymore; we are now using the past to help us read Scripture better. Maybe that's what we should be doing all along, which brings me to my second point.

Second, this project undervalues Scripture. If Scripture is sufficient "so that the man of God may be complete, equipped for every good work" (2 Tim 3:16-17), what room is left for tradition? The Bible does not limit itself to some areas of our life: it is sufficient *for every good work*. It gives us all the tools we need to live for God in this world, including contemporary Western culture.[4] From this perspective, we see the value of tradition but will not overvalue it. Tradition is invaluable for helping us understand Scripture; it is invaluable for helping us to understand our own culture; and it is invaluable for helping us overcome blind spots in our lives, areas where we assume our culture is the way things ought to be. But if the Bible is sufficient, if it is a light for our path, then tradition gives us nothing we need that we do not already have. We can see these issues more clearly if we examine one prominent example of ressourcement today, classical education.

B. Classical Education

There is a ressourcement movement amidst higher education, a move to capture ancient Christian educational practices and perspectives for today,[5] but I want to consider the movement briefly within grade school education.[6] In 1947, Dorothy Sayers delivered a lecture entitled, "The Lost Tools of Learning."[7] In this lecture, Sayers introduced ancient Christian pedagogy as an answer to issues in her day. Years later, this ressourcement caught on in evangelical circles and "classical" schools, schools employing the ancient Trivium (or grammar, dialectic [or logic], and rhetoric) to offer a uniquely Christian education. One influential author argues for a curriculum based on the Trivium, Latin, and classical texts. In part, this movement is an attempt to address problems within the public school system, yet the emphasis upon a particular curriculum—a classical one—goes beyond a critique of the public school system. The classical education movement rejects the various

---

[4] See the rest of the volumes in this series, "God's Gifts for the Christian Life."

[5] Cf. Dockery and Morgan, *Christian Higher Education*; Schuchardt, *Media*.

[6] See Appendix 2, a review of *The Case for Classical Schools*.

[7] Dorothy Sayers, "The Lost Tools of Learning- Dorothy Sayers," *Association of Classical Christian Schools (ACCS)*, January 5, 2017, accessed June 6, 2020, https://classicalchristian.org/the-lost-tools-of-learning-dorothy-sayers/.

approaches to learning that emerged throughout the Enlightenment and Postmodernism. Premodernism is seen as the answer to Postmodern tensions, and its expression in Classical education is explicitly seen as a significant way to save the West.[8] What should we make of this movement? In Appendix 2, I offer a review of one book arguing for this approach, and as the Lord grants me the opportunity, I hope to finish several projects on education that will give an opportunity for a more thorough interaction. For now, we can apply what we said above generally to this specific ressourcement.

What reason do we have for believing that Premodern answers to questions are better than Postmodern ones? Wilson tries to ground the Trivium in scripture, but his argument forces the text to say something it does not. If it is not biblical, what standard do we use to measure its value? Pragmatically, it seems to work and a lot of other methods fail, yet there are exceptions. Based on the social sciences, there are lots of approaches to education offered today. Each needs to be evaluated closely, but there is much good among it all. This research has some empirical basis, so it is better than the anecdotal evidence offered by Wilson. If we turn to philosophical theory, the philosophy at the root of Classical education is full of problems, and Modernism and Postmodernism have genuinely helped us understand our world better. So, on these grounds, Classical Education does not have a *prima facie* advantage over alternate approaches. Postmodern answers could be—and I believe in some regard are—better than Premodern ones.[9]

But as Christians we are primarily concerned with what Scripture teaches us, only secondarily with insights we gain by applying the Scriptures to our world. Biblically, there is no good reason to adopt a classical curriculum—though there are good biblical reasons for rejecting public schools. Many epistemological insights of Modernism and Postmodernism

---

[8] This association is clear in, Veith, *Post Christian*; Wilson, *The Case for Classical Christian Education.*

[9] Cf. Cornelius Van Til, *Essays on Christian Education* (Phillipsburg: The Presbyterian and Reformed Publishing Company, 1979). Van Til is essentially Postmodern in that he emphasizes the subject's participation in knowing, yet he is firmly in the realm of biblical Orthodoxy. Wilson incorporates Van Til's insights into his work but adopts an overall approach that developed within a worldview which is itself not compatible (in my opinion) with Van Til's best insights.

fit within the biblical teaching more than Premodernism,[10] so a theory and practice of education built upon those insights that derive from or cohere with the Bible will provide better answers to our problems than Premodern ones. The point is this: ressourcement only has value if it is grounded in Scripture, but at this point, why not just turn to the Scriptures and see what they say instead of adapting ancient answers for today's questions? This brings us to a third strategy, also a ressourcement of sorts.

C. Strategic Retreat

A few years back, the book *The Benedict Option* was causing waves among the Evangelical community.[11] Its author offered a ressourcement of the ancient Benedictine monastic order. As the monks survived the social upheaval of the Fall of Rome and the so-called Dark Ages, so we could survive the upheavals of Western society through a strategic retreat. By forming close-knit communities, analogous to the monasteries yet not physically isolated, Christianity can preserve its identity through the demise of the West. In his book *Post Christian,* Gene Veith suggests adapting Dreher's position within a more Protestant-friendly analogy than monasticism. For Veith, a strategic retreat may be a way to preserve Christian identity *and* Western culture.

> Today, some Christians are urging that the church approach our post-Christian times as the early church approached the Dark Ages: pull back from the collapsing culture; separate from the barbarians; keep learning alive and preserve our cultural heritage; build up our Christian institutions (the church, the family, schools, local communities). And someday, maybe, the church will convert the barbarians and bring civilisation back to life.[12]
>
> When it comes to education, Christians may be in exactly the same position as the church in the Dark Ages: preserving literacy, transmitting knowledge, and saving civilisation. And if Christians

---

[10] Cf. Rutherford, *The Gift of Knowing.*

[11] Rod Dreher, *The Benedict Option: A Strategy for Christians in a Post-Christian Nation* (New York, New York: Sentinel, 2017).

[12] Veith, *Post Christian,* 225.

become better educated than their secularist peers—if they can think objectively, creatively, with knowledge and the capacity to build on the discoveries of the past—who will be the leaders and culture-makers in the decades ahead?[13]

Yet, as we have seen, there is no biblical reason to try and save the West. Moreover, bigger issues are clear in these approaches.

As one reviewer of Dreher's book observes, "Strategic Retreat" ignores the thrust of the New Testament teaching. Christians are not called to preserve an identity; they are called to be on mission, seeking to save the lost.[14] As I wrote in a Gospel Coalition article, the current state of society may very well be an opportunity for the Gospel to go forth clearly.[15] Strategic retreat is better than all-out retreat, but what are we trying to preserve that the Bible commands us to preserve? And what would we lose in the process? Will we not lose the opportunities God has given us right here and now to manifest his kingdom and shine forth as a city on a hill? As with the ressourcements above, we are also faced with the question of warrant: why ought we do this? How do we know we ought to? What standard are we turning to? The biblical case for retreat, strategic or not, is wanting; instead, we are called to make the best use of the time we have, for tomorrow is not guaranteed (Eph 5:16, 2 Pet 3:8-13); we are to endure suffering and trial in faithfulness to Christ (Rom 5:1-5; James 1:12-15; Rev 2:9-11, 17, 26-29, 3:3-6, 11-13, 22:12-15); and we are not to withdraw from the world, for then we would fail to be the witnesses we are called to be (John 17:14-19, 1 Cor 5:9-13). Ressourcement of these sorts is not the only approach to contemporary culture, to saving the West, adopted by Christians. Ressourcement is generally a way of counteracting the influence of what is seen as negative in contemporary culture; it affirms the need to engage with and overcome contemporary culture. It is a strategy that fits well within several broader models of Christian cultural engagement. Though Classical Schools are often seen as part of transformationalist agenda, they are equally compatible with an Anabaptist vision of radical separation or Dreher and Veith's Christian

---

[13] Ibid., 227.

[14] Joshua Hollmann, "Christian Witness in the Present: Charles Taylor, Secularism, and The Benedict Option," *Concordia Journal* 46, no. 1 (2020): 57–67.

[15] Rutherford, "Benefits of Secularity."

counterculture. In the next two chapters, I want to turn from specific tactics to broader models of Christian cultural engagement. In the next chapter, I want to consider the transformationalist or Neo-Calvinist model, which affirms the value of culture but believes it is the Church's task to transform secular culture into a Christendom. Then, in chapter 6, we will consider the Reformed two kingdoms (R2K) model, which affirms the value of culture and attributes to it a separate domain than the church.

5

WE SAVE THE WEST BY TRANSFORMING IT

With the Edict of Milan (313), a profound shift took place in Western culture. Almost overnight, Christianity turned from being a persecuted sect to the dominate cultural force in the Roman Empire. Disagreement abounds over Constantine's motivations, but many see the beginnings of the first Christendom (to be secured under Theodosius) as a triumph of Christianity and an exemplar of faithful Christian presence. A dominant view among Evangelicalism today, often among those of a Reformed persuasion or tradition, is what I am calling "transformationalism."[1] transformationalism believes that Christians are called not only to give witness for the Gospel in the world but also to expand Christ's physical kingdom on earth by living in a distinctly Christian manner and setting up distinctly Christian institutions, including governments. Timothy Keller identifies its governing motif as *"thinking and living in all areas of life in a distinctively Christian manner."*[2] Douglas Wilson, for example, calls for the establishment of a "mere Christendom," nations that are defined by the confession of the Lordship of Christ.

Wilson appeals to the great commission to argue for his approach, "Go

---

[1] In Niebuhr's taxonomy, transformationalism is one possible manifestation of the "Christ Above Culture" view, a manifestation he calls "Christ the Transformer of Culture." Cf. the discussion in Carson, *Christ and Culture Revisited*, 15–25.

[2] Keller, *Center Church*, 235.

forth and baptise all *nations*." For various reasons, discussed below and in appendix 1, I do not think this is a correct interpretation of the text, but others present a more compelling argument for this position by appealing to the so-called "cultural mandate" and to a postmillennial eschatology. For the rest of this chapter, we will consider transformationalism through the lens of these two doctrines.

A. The Cultural Mandate[3]

According to Cornelius Plantinga, the cultural mandate is a commission to not only "care for earth and animals ('subduing' what's already there) but also [to develop] certain cultural possibilities ('filling' out what is only potentially there)."[4] This is, of course, drawing on the language of God's commission to Adam in the early chapters of Genesis. Transformationalists believe that this mandate continues after the Fall, now the task of renewing the creation and fallen human culture.[5] In its original form, God commanded Adam to "be fruitful and multiply, fill the earth and put it under subjection; rule over the fish of sea, the birds of the heavens, and over all the living creatures that crawl upon the earth" (Gen 1:28).[6] Read in the context of Genesis and the unfolding biblical story, this mandate is seen as a command to imitate God in his creative act and to rule over the earth as God's vice-regents.[7]

God's commission to Adam is often called the "cultural mandate"

---

[3] My discussion of the Cultural Mandate is adapted from an essay I wrote a few years ago on the subject, "Appendix 2: Christ and Culture." Https://teleioteti.ca/papers.

[4] Cornelius Plantinga, *Engaging God's World: A Christian Vision of Faith, Learning, and Living* (Grand Rapids: Eerdmans, 2002), 33. Cf. C. Gregg Singer, "A Philosophy of History," in *Jerusalem and Athens: Critical Discussions on the Theology and Apologetics of Cornelius Van Til*, ed. E. R. Geehan (Phillipsburg: Presbyterian and Reformed Publishing Co., 1971), 331; Van Til, *The Calvinistic Concept of Culture*, 27; Frame, *The Doctrine of the Christian Life*, 270.

[5] Louis Berkhof, *Systematic Theology* (Grand Rapids: Eerdmans, 1996), 499–500.

[6] My translation.

[7] G. K. Beale, *A New Testament biblical Theology: The Unfolding of the Old Testament in the New* (Grand Rapids: Baker Academic, 2011), 384.

because cultural artifacts, the objects and structures of human creative endeavour, are seen to be the fulfillment of this mandate. We imitate God by creating new ways of living within, interacting with, and employing the created order; we rule this order by unfolding its potential to give glory to God. This understanding of the mandate is reflected, transformationalists argue, in the creative works of Cain's descendants, recorded in Genesis 4.[8] The purpose of this mandate is to expand God's kingdom on earth for the glory of his name. The work of Cain's descendants is thus a perversion of this original intent, an extension of man's glory and purposes instead of God's.[9] This is where the element of transformation or renewal becomes necessary. By producing new cultural products and overturning the fallen works of unredeemed humanity, by transforming the culture's of this world into truly Christian cultures—or Christendom—Christians fulfil this original mandate.[10] A Christian, a citizen of God's kingdom inaugurated through Jesus, "should see all of life and all of reality in light of the goal of the redemption of the cosmos."[11]

I have benefitted greatly from the work of these scholars and am convinced by their interpretation of God's original commission to Adam as a command to rule and develop God's kingdom on earth. The kingdom of God is one of the most significant themes throughout the Bible, both in the Old and New Testaments,[12] and the case that it begins here is compelling. For this reason, I prefer to call it "the kingdom mandate," especially since

---

[8] Bruce K. Waltke and Charles Yu, *An Old Testament Theology: An Exegetical, Canonical, and Thematic Approach*, 1st ed. (Grand Rapids: Zondervan, 2007), 220.

[9] Frame, *The Doctrine of the Christian Life*, 863; Cornelius Van Til, "Part 3-- A. The Dilemma of Education," in *Essays on Christian Education* (Phillipsburg: The Presbyterian and Reformed Publishing Company, 1979).

[10] Cf. Frame, *The Doctrine of the Christian Life*, 874; Berkhof, *Systematic Theology*, 499–500.

[11] Anthony A Hoekema, *The Bible and the Future*, Revised, Reprint. (Grand Rapids: Eerdmans, 1994), 54.

[12] Cf. Stephen G. Dempster, *Dominion and Dynasty: A biblical Theology of the Hebrew Bible*, New Studies in biblical Theology 15 (Leicester: Downers Grove: Apollos; InterVarsity, 2003); J. Alexander Rutherford, *God's Kingdom through His Priest-King: An Analysis of the Book of Samuel in Light of the Davidic Covenant*, Teleioteti Technical Studies 1 (Vancouver: Teleioteti, 2019).

"culture" is an ambiguous term, and the kingdom mandate is never explicitly associated in the Bible with cultural products. However, I am not so convinced that the mandate continues after the Fall in the manner the transformationalists argue it does. After the Fall, the kingdom mandate becomes a strategy in what we could call cosmic warfare: it is the way God's people are to expand God's kingdom over against the hostile kingdom of Satan. The outcome of this war is prefigured in Genesis 3:15, where God curses the serpent, "I will put enmity between you and the woman, and between your offspring and her offspring; he shall bruise your head, and you shall bruise his heel." Here the conflict between these two kingdoms is shown to find its end in the victory of the woman's son over Satan's offspring.[13] The success of Cain's descendants in establishing cities and tools for subduing the earth represents an early advance in the kingdom of Satan. Indeed, by the days of Noah, the whole earth appears to be under his dominion. The first inklings of hope in the birth of Seth seem to have disappeared, yet God acts through the flood to wipe out the efforts of this earthly kingdom of Satan and preserve the righteous Noah and his children. The kingdom of Satan finds its immediate realization in Noah's children and at Babel.[14] God recommissions Noah to multiply his kingdom, in Genesis 9, but without a clear strategy for victory, Satan's kingdom appears to be dominant on earth.

In Genesis 12, the language of the kingdom mandate appears again. This chapter gives us an idea of how God will fulfil his promise to crush the Serpent. Here, he promises to multiply Abraham's descendants and fill the earth with them (12:1-2, 17:6). Significantly, he promises to bring forth kings from Abraham's descendants and bless all the earth through his offspring, whom Paul interprets to be Jesus (Gen 17:6; cf. Gal 3:8-9, 15-22). The narratives of Noah and Abraham demonstrate how inept God's people are

---

[13] "Offspring" is a collective noun in Hebrew. It is clear from the singular pronoun and the rest of Scripture that the offspring of woman is Jesus, but the offspring of Satan is all humanity who follows in his rebellion against God.

[14] Babel and the related name Babylon become a symbol of Satan's kingdom throughout Scripture, in contrast with Jerusalem, the symbol of God's kingdom. Cf. T. Desmond Alexander, *The City of God and the Goal of Creation*, Short Studies in biblical Theology (Wheaton: Crossway, 2018); J. Alexander Rutherford, "Review of The City of God and the Goal of Creation," *Teleioteti*, March 8, 2018, accessed March 24, 2020, https://teleioteti.ca/2018/03/08/review-of-the-city-of-god-and-the-goal-of-creation/. (See Appendix 3.)

to fulfil his purposes: if his kingdom is going to expand on earth, it will have to be his work that accomplishes it.[15] Up to this point, the kingdom mandate is something God will fulfil. This hardly lends support to the contention that this is something God's people can and will fulfil through their earthly actions. When God acts through Moses to set up an earthly kingdom, the stewards to which he entrusts repeatedly fail to steward this kingdom well. Their failure results in the exile of God's people amidst Satan's kingdom—in Babylon. The Old Testament ends with God's people scattered in hostile territory and no indication when God will bring about his promised Messiah, the one who will fulfil God's promise to crush the Serpent.

In the New Testament, Jesus is seen to be the focus of all of God's promises; he is the offspring who will bring an end to Satan's kingdom. This victory is guaranteed through Jesus' earthly ministry, crucifixion, and resurrection, yet it is oddly left unfinished. Jesus has bound the strong man, booted him out of heaven, and severely restricted his activity (Mark 3:27; Luke 10:18-20; John 12:31, 16:11; Col 2:15; Rev 12:9, 20:1-3). However, we are told that Satan will be released one day in the future, that his kingdom is still strong on the earth (Rev 20:1-3; Eph 2:1-2, 6:10-20; 2 Cor 4:1-6; 1 Pet 5:8), and that his decisive defeat will only come when Christ returns. We are even said to take part in this: "The God of peace will soon crush Satan under your feet" (Rom 16:20). What Paul commands of the Romans in context—throughout the book—is not cultural works but "the obedience of faith," or works that correspond to the faith that has saved them. Indeed, Romans begins with the kingdom of God and ends with the kingdom of God: Paul starts with the kingdom established by God through Christ, a son of David (Rom 1:3-6), and ends with this statement that God will achieve victory under the feet of his people (16:20). Both chapters also tie Paul's ministry to the gentiles in general, and so to the Romans, with the goal of attaining "the obedience of faith" (Rom 1:5, 16:26). From this alone, it would appear that God will accomplish the kingdom mandate ultimately with the return of his Son but for now through the spreading of the Gospel and the building up of the church. This is confirmed by the only clear allusion to the kingdom mandate in the New Testament.

In Matthew 28, Jesus gives his disciples the "great commission."

---

[15] Rutherford, *God's Kingdom*.

Because "All authority in heaven and on earth" has been given to Jesus, his people must go "and make disciples of all nations, baptizing them in the name of the Father and of the Son and of the Holy Spirit, teaching them to observe all that I have commanded you. And behold, I am with you always, to the end of the age" (18-20).[16] Instead of a command to subdue and rule, we are told that Christ is ruling and has subdued: he has all authority. This is consistent with the testimony of Mark, Luke, John, Colossians, and Revelation, cited above. Jesus entrusts the task of multiplying to his disciples; they are to go forth to make disciples. That they are to go to all nations echoes God's promise to Abraham, that through his offspring all nation will be blessed (Gen 12:1-3; cf. Gal 3:1-29, esp. 3:8). The kingdom mandate is thus seen to be in an "already-not-yet" tension in the New Testament. Christ has secured victory over Satan and his kingdom, yet that victory is not yet fully enacted. Jesus will return and deliver the final blow, but until that time, God's people are to progressively expand his kingdom on earth. They are not to do this by building culture and transforming society, which the New Testament never once commands. Instead, they are to do so by making disciples and teaching them obedience, the same thing we saw in Romans.

So, with transformationalists, we ought to see continuity between the kingdom mandate given to Adam and our current labours on earth. However, as we have seen and will see further in Part 3, this labour is not cultural labour but labour to see the Church spread across the globe. In addition to the cultural mandate, many transformationalists also find confirmation of their view in the logic of postmillennial eschatology.[17]

B. The Postmillennial Vision

Postmillennialism is the doctrine that this world will get progressively better

---

[16] John Frame is an example of a transformationalist who sees the relationship between the great commission and the cultural mandate, but he does not acknowledge the transformation of the original commission seen in the great commission. Frame, *The Doctrine of the Christian Life*, 203, 310. Cf. David L. Turner, *Matthew*, Baker Exegetical Commentary on the New Testament (Grand Rapids: Baker Academic, 2008), 691.

[17] Cf. Appendix 1.

until it is wholly identified with the Kingdom of God, at which point Christ will return to rule in a bodily fashion. The New Creation thus describes the renewed creation; there will be continuity between the world we experience now and the world that will soon come. In this way, postmillennialism has a profoundly positive view of the progression of the Gospel throughout the world; God's kingdom will assuredly expand. Though his kingdom will not be fully realized before his return, "Christian principles will be the rule, not the exception," and "Christ will return to a truly Christianized world."[18] As Douglas Wilson describes it, this does not mean that there will be a continuous line of advance: there may be at times steps back into darkness. However, when viewed in the context of the whole, there will always be progress towards the future reign of God on earth.[19]

Like amillennialism, postmillennialism understands the millennial reign of Christ in Revelation 20:1-6 to be figurative, referring to the current reign of Christ. However, postmillennialism distinguishes itself with the belief that Christ's heavenly reign will be embodied on earth before his return and that there will be continuity between the present creation and the world to come. It is obvious how postmillennialism fits into the transformationalist view: if Christ's kingdom will be manifest on earth and continuity will be maintained, then cultural labours and earthly engagement with kingdoms now will have enduring, eternal consequences. We can participate in spreading his kingdom by reforming earthly governments and our cultural labours will endure into the New Creation. All our labours in this life will have eternal consequences, therefore. "The changed character of individuals will be reflected in an uplifted social, economic, political and cultural life of mankind."[20]

To support this view, Douglas Wilson and Lorraine Boettner both appeal to Matthew 28:18-20: "We believe that the Great Commission includes not merely the formal and external announcement of the Gospel preached as a 'witness' to the nations… but the true and effectual evangelization of all the nations so that the hearts and lives of the people are

---

[18] Loraine Boettner, "Postmillennialism," in *The Meaning of the Millennium: Four Views*, ed. George Eldon Ladd and Robert G. Clouse (Downers Grove: InterVarsity Press, 1977), 118.

[19] In *Empires of Dirt*. Cf. Appendix 1.

[20] Boettner, "Postmillennialism," 117.

transformed by it."²¹ As I argue in Appendix 1, this loads more onto this passage than it can bear. Jesus' commission means that all peoples of the earth ought to hear the Gospel and believe—and many in fact do—but it does not guarantee the proportion of people who will believe (such that a majority will) nor that socio-political nations will be converted. Boettner argues from the contrasting pictures of heaven (a city full of thousands of thousands) and hell (a lake or pit) that Heaven will be far greater in the scope of its inhabitants.²² This may be true, though Jesus does specify that the way into his kingdom is hard and the gate narrow, few find it (Matt 7:13-14). However, there is little other New Testament exegetical support for this view, at least in its political implications.

One may appeal to the pictures in the Old Testament prophets of the nations being blessed and kings streaming to Jerusalem to offer their gifts to God (Isa 60:3, 5, 11). One difficulty of appealing to Old Testament texts in this regard is that the Old Testament has what we could call a collapsed eschatology. There is no or very little distinction between the first and second coming of Christ in the Old Testament. The whole period from Christ's first coming to his return and the new creation is presented as the eschatological realization of God's rule on earth. This means that some of this imagery was fulfilled in Christ's first coming (such as the magi bringing him gifts), during the Church age (the Gentiles coming to faith), and at his return (the resurrection of the dead, defeat of sin, and the end of conflict and death). Douglas Wilson appeals to texts in Revelation to support this view, namely that kings would enter the gates of the New Jerusalem (Rev 21:24) and the leaves of the trees in the New Jerusalem "were for the healing of the nations" (Rev 22:2). However, this imagery actually supports reading the physical language of nations and kings coming to Jesus in the Old Testament as being fulfilled in the salvation of the Gentiles. In the context of Revelation 19-22, the New Jerusalem is not identified as a physical city but as the people of God, the bride of Christ, prepared in all her glory (Rev 21:2, 9-10; cf. Eph 5:32). Beale is surely right when he writes that "healing" here refers to the removal of the curse and eternal life and that "nations" indicates that this healing is "for all peoples throughout the world who have believed the gospel." It is not for socio-political units but all peoples, Jews and gentiles

---

²¹ Ibid., 118.

²² Ibid., 124.

alike.²³ Concerning the kings bringing their "glory," this most likely refers to worship and so likewise paints the picture of believers from all nations of the earth, and of all socio-economic statuses in this world, coming before God in the new creation to worship him.²⁴ The transformation of what appears to be literal, physical language in the Old Testament here in the New should caution us against an overly literal reading of the Old Testament prophets, a caution that also arises from studying the way the prophetic books communicate in other passages.²⁵

C. Conclusion

Without evidence of a continuing cultural mandate as taught by transformationalists and without the support of a postmillennial eschatology, there is no good theological or biblical-theological reason to adhere to this view. This affirms the already glaring lack of explicit exegetical evidence warranting cultural transformation. Indeed, this may be the most significant argument against such a view. If Scripture is truly sufficient for the Christian life—so that the "man of God may be complete, equipped for every good work" (2 Tim 3:17)—it is truly conspicuous that no instructions are given for engaging transformationally or redemptively with culture.

Given the evidence for an alternate approach to cultural engagement, as has already been suggested thus far in this book and will be brought together in Part 3, we ought not to adopt a transformationalist view. We cannot and ought not to save the West by transforming it.

---

[23] G.K. Beale, *The Book of Revelation: A Commentary on the Greek Text*, NIGTC (Grand Rapids; Carlisle: Eerdmans; Paternoster, 1999), 1107–1108.

[24] Ibid., 1094–1096.

[25] Cf. J. Alexander Rutherford, *The Gift of Reading - Part 1: Reading the Bible in Submission to God*, God's Gifts for the Christian Life Part 1 Vol. 2a (Vancouver: Teleioteti, 2019), 150–155.

6

WE LIVE IN THE WEST AS GOOD CITIZENS

We may not be able to save the West by transforming it according to a Christian standard, but may we nevertheless save it by living within it according to its own logic? That is, if Christians cannot reform society and culture by the Bible, may they not transform it by natural law? Such a possibility is opened by the Reformed Two Kingdoms (R2K) doctrine.

In his book *Natural Law and the Two Kingdoms*,[1] David VanDrunen argues that the Two Kingdoms view of Christian cultural engagement has strong historical pedigree, stretching from Augustine through Calvin to its modern proponents.[2] More recently, this doctrine has been given new life through the work of Meredith Kline,[3] VanDrunen,[4] and similar thinkers.

---

[1] David VanDrunen, *Living in God's Two Kingdoms: A biblical Vision for Christianity and Culture* (Crossway, 2010).

[2] The two kingdoms should not be confused with Augustine's two cities, the City of Man and the City of God. This later antithesis is one of opposition and warfare: it corresponds better to the antithesis I am drawing between the kingdom of Satan expressed through fallen humanity and the kingdom of God expressed through the Church. Augustine, *Saint Augustine: The City of God*, vol. 7, p. . Cf. VanDrunen, *Living in God's Two Kingdoms*, 14 ft. 3; Alexander, *The City of God and the Goal of Creation*; Rutherford, "Review of The City of God and the Goal of Creation."

[3] Cf. Meredith G. Kline, "Kingdom Prologue," 1993.

[4] See Appendix 3 for my review of VanDrunen's *Living in God's Two Kingdoms*; this book will be the primary conversation partner for this view.

Keller identifies the governing motif for Christian cultural engagement within the two kingdoms view as "the importance of doing [secular] work in a way marked by an excellence that all can see."[5] As the name implies, the R2K position holds that there are two kingdoms at work in the world. It may be better to think of "kingdoms" in this position as "dispensations" or "economies": by "kingdom," R2K proponents do not mean an organized socio-political structure with a king, a people, and land but a manner in which God governs people on earth.[6]

The first kingdom is the "Common Kingdom," the kingdom that believers and unbelievers both partake of. According to VanDrunen, this kingdom is given official sanction from God in his covenant with Noah (Genesis 9): the command to be fruitful and multiply and the instructions concerning retributive justice establish the common institutions of the state and the family.[7]

The second kingdom is the "Redemptive Kingdom," established through God's covenant with Abraham. The Redemptive Kingdom is God's instrument for about his original destiny for humanity, life and fellowship with him in the "world-to-come."[8] Both of these kingdoms have co-existed on earth since the time of Abraham. Like Abraham and the Babylonian exiles, Christians live with a foot in both kingdoms. When Israel lived within the land of Israel, the common kingdom was not in effect for their life and practice. Instead, all life was governed under the redemptive kingdom. However, when they left the land, the two kingdoms were again in effect.[9] In these cases, for the exiles and Christians, their religious and private life (in the sense of actions and conscience) are governed by God's redemptive

---

[5] Keller, *Center Church*, 235. This position corresponds with Niebuhrs "Christ and Culture in paradox." Cf. Carson, *Christ and Culture Revisited*, 15–25.

[6] Graeme Goldsworthy these three components as the essential pieces of a kingdom, at least as the concept is found in the Bible. *The Gospel and the Kingdom* in Graeme Goldsworthy, *The Goldsworthy Trilogy* (Milton Keynes: Paternoster, 2012), 53–54.

[7] VanDrunen, *Living in God's Two Kingdoms*, 78–81. In his *Kingdom Prologue*, Meredith Kline sees the institution of the state earlier, in Genesis 4 with God's mark given to Cain. Kline, "Kingdom Prologue."

[8] VanDrunen, *Living in God's Two Kingdoms*, 83–84.

[9] Ibid., 75–97.

covenants and the Scriptures; their public life, work in the "secular" (i.e. non-religious) realm, is governed by God's natural law.¹⁰ Both spheres are ordained by God, so they are good. However, R2K proponents acknowledge a spiritual antithesis in the world between believers and unbelievers. For this reason, the common kingdom is rife with conflict: unbelievers twist natural law to their own ends or dismiss it completely, and believers attempt to honour God with their conduct in the common realm (in the Family, state, and all other non-religious institutions (i.e. everywhere but the gathered church)).¹¹

We can identify three central, distinguishing marks of the R2K position over against transformationalism and the position developed in this book. First, like the transformationalist position, R2K proponents argue that non-religious labour and institutions have value. However, the R2K position rejects the abiding cultural mandate as the reasons for this. Instead, it is because God has instituted and blessed the common kingdom through his covenant with Noah that common labour and culture have value. Second, the common kingdom is not governed by God's special revelation but by natural law. This means, for example, that Theonomists would be wrong to apply the Mosaic Law to a contemporary Christendom¹² and that a similar attempt to make New Testament ethics normative for the state would also be misguided. As noted above, this does not mean that the Scriptures do not apply to the common kingdom; it means they apply indirectly, as they

---

[10] David VanDrunen, *A biblical Case for Natural Law* (The Action Institute, 2006), 37–39. VanDrunen clarifies in a blog post and in a more recent book that Scripture is normative for all life; as such, it informs the Christian opinion of the common kingdom. The natural law is normative for the common kingdom, "as Christians appeal to the natural law in the common kingdom, either to appeal to unbelievers or to try to understand their own responsibilities in various areas of life, they should look to Scripture to correct and clarify their views on natural law." David VanDrunen, "Two Kingdoms and Moral Standards," College, *Valiant for Truth*, February 28, 2011, https://web.archive.org/web/20120122080308/http:/wscal.edu/blog/entry/two-kingdoms-and-moral-standards; VanDrunen, *Living in God's Two Kingdoms*, chap. 7.

[11] VanDrunen, *Living in God's Two Kingdoms*, 76–78.

[12] Cf. Rousas J Rushdoony, *The Institutes of biblical Law*, 3 vols. (Phillipsburg: P & R Pub, 1973).

illumine for us the natural law by which God governs that kingdom. Third, the gathered church is the focus of the Redemptive Kingdom; thus, it is also the focus of the Christian life.[13] These three emphases give us a window into the argument for the R2K position and an avenue to critique it.

A. The Common Kingdom

VanDrunen argues against the transformationalist view by sketching a biblical theology of two Adams.[14] Essentially, he argues that the cultural mandate is no longer valid because Jesus fulfilled all that Adam was assigned to do and received all that Adam hoped to gain.[15] Instead of dismissing the value of common labours along with the cultural mandate, R2K proponents find continuing value for cultural labours in the institution of God's common kingdom. A preliminary issue emerges at this point; though VanDrunen and others assign worth to common labours, they cannot give a sufficient account (at least in my opinion) of that worth. Common labours do not contribute to anything of lasting value, for this age will pass away, nor do they further Christ's kingdom on earth, for his kingdom is spiritual and realized in the gathered church. What value is there, then, in common labours? All VanDrunen can say is that "Hard work, with God's blessing, is truly its own reward."[16] This is, however, pastorally and psychologically—and biblically—insufficient.

Pastorally, how can we give hope to a parishioner struggling with life in the common world if this all we can say? If they have not found their hard work to be its own reward, what more can we say to them? Psychologically, humans need purpose; the lack of purpose, such as is implied by this, is called "nihilism." Nihilism, of course, leads to despair. As much as we can criticize Greek literature, no one would look at Sisyphus and say that "hard work is its own reward."[17] Hard labour without any concrete purpose or achievement

---

[13] VanDrunen, *Living in God's Two Kingdoms*, 102–117.

[14] See Appendix 2.

[15] VanDrunen, *Living in God's Two Kingdoms*, 35–71.

[16] Ibid., 189.

[17] Sisyphus was sentenced to roll a heavy boulder up a hill only to have it roll to the bottom and repeat the process for eternity.

is hopeless, and it is this hopelessness that our society struggles with so much. Can we only add to this despair the assurance that God has blessed this labour? Biblically, I can see no ground for this teaching. For one, labour for labour's sake was not sufficient for Adam; God tasked him with labouring to build God's kingdom on earth, for his glory. Elsewhere in the Bible—as we will see later—this is the only enduring value given to common labour. The exegetical justification for the common kingdom does not make up for this serious deficiency, namely, the inability of the R2K position to give abiding value to common labour.

VanDrunen and other R2K proponents look to the early chapters of Genesis to find the institution of the common kingdom. However, upon closer examination, their argument does not withstand much scrutiny. For one, God's covenant with Noah does not instate something new but ratifies God's original covenant made with Adam with a renewed humanity, Noah and his descendants. Stephen Wellum and Peter Gentry argue this linguistically from the verb used in Genesis 9:9: God does not "cut" (כרת, *krt*) a covenant but "upholds" (קום, *kûm*) a covenant; the latter term, they argue, is used primarily for reaffirming a covenant that already exists.[18] In addition, this reaffirmation of the covenant echoes the language from God's original creation and commission of Adam: there is a command to "Be fruitful and multiply and fill the earth" (9:1; 1:22, 28), mention of the spheres of life originally put under Adam's rule (9:2; 1:28), an indication of God's provision for food (9:3; 1:29-30), and the image of God (9:6; 1:27). The allusions are clear; God has recommissioned Noah with Adam's commission. However, it is clear from Genesis that a post-fall reality is reflected: death is permissible, and justice is required for the life of humanity. VanDrunen makes much of the lack of religious provisions in the Noachene covenant, but it should be observed that there were none with Adam's covenant. The rest of Scripture applies the language of Adam in the garden to the temple and priesthood, but this does not mean that Adam was the first priest; it means that in the temple the garden is retained, if only in a symbolic fashion.[19]

---

[18] Peter John Gentry and Stephen J. Wellum, *Kingdom through Covenant: A Biblical-Theological Understanding of the Covenants* (Wheaton: Crossway, 2012).

[19] That is, we should read revelation diachronically; later texts draw their imagery from earlier texts, not vice versa.

Indeed, Noah recapitulates Adam's behaviour: he talks with God and plants his own garden, only to sin with the products of that garden as Adam and Eve originally did. So, something new is not instituted with the Noachene covenant.

The above connections also caution us against finding common kingdom institutions in this passage. The command to be fruitful and multiply is not the institution (or reinstitution) of the family but is the re-expression of God's initial command for humanity to spread his kingdom on earth. As for the state, the "*lex talionis*" (law of retaliation) provision says nothing about institutionalized justice, such as is expressed by the Mosaic or secular state. Indeed, in context, it would seem to command interpersonal not institutional justice, as is witnessed throughout the Old Testament—including the Torah provisions concerning the avenger of blood. Indeed, there is no clear implementation of the state here or elsewhere in Scripture (the Mosaic law, for example, entrusts the priesthood with significant aspects of civil justice and mediating disputes (e.g. Deut 17:8-13, 19:15-21, 21:1-9); though the kings and those the people appoint did this also (e.g. Deut 16:18-20; 2 Sam 15:1-6)).[20] I think it is telling that VanDrunen identifies the authority structures of the state and family as *implications* derived through natural law from the basic institution of justice and family. The point is this: there is no explicit biblical mandate for the state or family structure as they are found in the common kingdom.[21] It is true that Romans 13 tells us to submit to earthly authorities and that they are instituted by God, but this is insufficient to uphold the claims for the R2K common kingdom. This does not say that God instituted these structures according to natural law or that they have his stamp of approval; it means that he uses them to achieve a good purpose on earth. The same relationship is witnessed throughout the Old Testament when God uses utterly depraved kingdoms, like Babylon, to further his good purposes (e.g. Hab 1:5). The point is this: though it is true that family and government are institutions shared in common between believers and unbelievers, there is no indication in the Bible that God has blessed these institutions for their own sake nor that these institutions are

---

[20] John Frame argues that the idea of state is an evolution of the family structure. Frame, *The Doctrine of the Christian Life*, 595–602.

[21] Cf. VanDrunen, *Living in God's Two Kingdoms*, 153.

governed by God's natural law. This brings us to the troubles with natural law.

B. Natural Law

Natural law has received extensive discussion over the years, so we will have to be somewhat narrow in our discussion. We will focus on natural law as it is found in Christian ethics, particularly that of R2K; for this reason, we will employ VanDrunen's definition for our discussion here. In his book *Divine Covenants and Moral Order: A biblical Theology of Natural Law*, VanDrunen identifies the natural law as basic moral boundaries God has embedded in the natural order. It does not contain, for example, a "detailed political system" but provides the "basic moral boundaries within which responsible human agents can develop concrete legal systems."[22] That is, natural law gives a basic order, not discrete rules.[23] It is not a "*distinctively Christian* ethic, for it places all people under obligation to God not *as Christians* but *as human beings* (though Christians carry out their natural law responsibilities as part of their obedience to Christ)."[24] This law is "natural" because it corresponds "with the nature with which he made them." It is law because it is legal: it involves justice and a moral standard.[25] It is a "natural moral order" that provides an ethic for "a richer way of life that promotes a modest human flourishing in the fallen world, and which also reminds human beings of their ultimate accountability before God and his judgment."[26] This corresponds with J. Budziszewski's definition of natural law as "moral principles that are both right for everybody and knowable to everybody by the ordinary exercise of human reason."[27] I do not want to suggest in this chapter that there is no value in the concept of natural law; on the contrary,

---

[22] David VanDrunen, *Divine Covenants and Moral Order: A biblical Theology of Natural Law*, Emory University studies in law and religion (Grand Rapids: Eerdmans, 2014), 26.

[23] Ibid., 25.

[24] Ibid., 486.

[25] Ibid., 481.

[26] Ibid., 481, 483.

[27] Quoted in Frame, *The Doctrine of the Christian Life*, 243.

it is clear that God has revealed himself to his creation and that there is a moral order to the creation he has made. However, it is one thing to acknowledge this and another to suggest that natural law can function apart from Scripture or verbal revelation. After considering some of the biblical evidence for natural law, I want to then consider the broader problem using a non-verbal revelation, or the created order, to establish ethical norms (what is often called the naturalistic fallacy).

In his book *Divine Covenants and Moral Order*, VanDrunen suggests that natural law is implied throughout Scripture, but in this book and his *Living in God's Two Kingdoms*, he employs two specific texts to make this point, Genesis 20 and Romans 1:18-2:16.[28] In Genesis 20, Abraham finds himself at tension with Abimelech, king of Gerar. VanDrunen contends that we see natural law implied in this text because of Abimelech's behaviour: he acknowledges the moral impropriety of taking another's wife and employs the judicial category of innocence to defend his people.[29] Unlike Sodom and Gomorrah, "Abimelech and Gerar recognize [the baseline natural obligations of the Noahic covenant] and, to some degree, submit to them."[30] In this case, and in his other appeals to the Old Testament narratives, the texts do not prove VanDrunen's point. If we had reason to believe in natural law from elsewhere in Scripture, we could use the concept to explain what is going on here; however, apart from such teaching, these texts cannot be used to demonstrate the doctrine. Natural law is neither the only nor the best explanation for what is going on in this text. We can offer several other possibilities that are as equally plausible or more so. First, Genesis portrays a world were God remains active in speaking with his people, with those who "fear God." Not only does he communicate explicitly with Abraham but he also communicates through a dream with Abimelech (Gen 20:6-7) and in many ways to Job, though Abraham is the only person with whom he enters a covenant to fulfil his redemptive purpose.[31] In addition to these explicit

---

[28] Cf. VanDrunen, *Divine Covenants and Moral Order*, 483; VanDrunen, *Living in God's Two Kingdoms*, 86.

[29] VanDrunen, *Divine Covenants and Moral Order*, 149–154.

[30] Ibid.

[31] There is debate over the historicity of Job, but the rest of Scripture treats Job as a historical figure and the story of his life is set in the Patriarchal period.

accounts of God's communication, we are also told that Melchizedek is a "priest of God Most High" (Gen 14:18). This is clearly a positive attribution and indicates that there is redemptive knowledge of God throughout the world; if there is sufficient knowledge for this king to worship and serve God, knowledge that is by definition not natural law (which deals only with ethical boundaries), how can we be sure that verbal, moral revelation is not known throughout Abraham's world? For example, in God's covenant with Noah, the foundational tenet of justice—*lex talionis*—is not presented as a feature of the natural order; instead, it is instituted by divine command. From this verbal revelation, many ethical implications could be drawn. Second, Roman's tells us that every person in the world knows God (Rom 1:18ff); we will discuss this passage below, but for now we can observe that knowledge of God sufficient to trigger the conscience is itself sufficient to explain the moral sense displayed by Abimelech in this passage. To respond as he does, Abimelech only has to have a sense of morality that is somewhat correct; he does not have to possess a moral ethic that has a normative basis in God's moral order. The point is this: texts like this avail themselves of many explanations. Natural law is far from the most obvious explanation.

In Romans 1:18-2:16, Paul presents the Gospel against the background of God's wrath against all humanity. All humans know God and are accountable for their idolatry, taking what they know of God and applying it to the created order. VanDrunen argues that this passage affirms a minimalist ethic, or basic ethical boundaries, evident to humanity within the created order.[32] There are many implications to be drawn from this passage, and I attempt to draw out some of these in this series ("God's Gifts for the Christian Life"), but natural law is not one of them. That is, Romans 1:18-2:16 demonstrates that all humanity is guilty because they know God and twist that knowledge in wilful rebellion, engaging in actions they knew to be sinful. There is some basic moral knowledge implied in this law. The appeal to nature in this passage (and in 1 Corinthians 10) affirms that there is something normative about God's created order. However, to function as VanDrunen would have it within the common kingdom, this revelation needs to function normatively without verbal revelation. This is something the text simply does not tell us. It does not say that humans could formulate ethical

---

[32] Cf. VanDrunen, *Divine Covenants and Moral Order*, chap. 5.

laws and determine the right behaviour in specific situations. More importantly, it does not say that when confronted by the immediate knowledge of the wrongness of their actions, they *could give a coherent reason why it is wrong*. The latter would be the case if natural law were taught in this passage, but Romans simply does not tell us that this is possible. If we consider the nature of ethical laws, we see that this is only possible if we have verbal revelation.

That is, to identify what parts and aspects of the moral order are ethically normative, we need someone to tell us. Solomon in the Proverbs is able to present the ant as an example of hard work (Prov 30:25), but he must know beforehand that hard work is an ethical virtue. Otherwise, a sluggard or glutton could come along and hold up the Koala as the model for work; we should eat for hours and then sleep the rest of the time. Only because we know that hard work is virtuous can we find in the ant an illustration of that virtue. The same goes for most fundamental virtues. If we look at the moral order as we know it, it is rife with death. The animal world gives some support to the idea of cold-hearted neglect for life in order to achieve a desired end—such as survival. However, with the biblical lens of the Fall, we can look at the world and find illustrations of mercy and self-sacrifice. Only with verbal revelation can we identify one aspect of the moral order as virtuous and another as a vice. For example, Roman Catholics often argue from the natural connection between sex and conception that contraception is sinful. However, the Bible, in the Song of Songs for example, suggests that sex is not only for conception but rightfully has pleasure as an end. We would have to know beforehand that the natural connection between sex and conception is a normative one to use it as an ethical norm. This is something that simply cannot be shown. We can generally argue, with Budziszewski, that the natural order is purposeful, allowing us to identify ethical truths within the natural order:

> An 'is' which merely 'happens to be' has no moral significance because it is arbitrary; that's why it cannot imply an 'ought.' But an 'is' which expresses the purposes of the Creator is fraught with an 'ought' already. Such are the inbuilt features of our design,

including the design of deep conscience.[33]

However, in specific cases, it is impossible to show that it is intended to be normative: "in the argument against contraception and in other arguments, it is difficult to show that the proposed restriction is in fact a law of God."[34] John Frame concludes from this, rightly I believe, that natural law is useful for apologetics but cannot be used to establish any ethical standards apart from the Bible: "If one presents a natural-law argument to someone who does not believe in natural law, who keeps challenging the authority on which the law is based, ultimately the argument must have recourse to Scripture. So natural-law arguments ultimately depend on arguments from Scripture."[35] In his *Living in God's Two Kingdoms,* VanDrunen argues from the workplace values shared by Christians and non-Christians alike that there is no uniquely Christian work ethic.[36] This may be the case, but one can imagine—and some of us have experienced—work situations where the ethics of punctuality and hard work are not well regarded. How could we argue for these virtues? We could appeal to profit, yet this does not establish them as ethical virtues only pragmatic virtues. There is no way to argue on the basis of the natural order alone that these are virtues. Believers and unbelievers alike may intuitively recognize them as virtuous, and we believers have biblical testimony that they are so, but apart from that verbal revelation, one cannot reason that they are. The inability for natural law on its own to act as ethically normative (in the positive sense) coupled with the spiritual antithesis puts common kingdom life on unstable ground: "the rather precarious status of general revelation in the nonbeliever's consciousness calls in question the likelihood of that revelation producing a stable moral consensus in modern secular culture sufficient to govern nations."[37]

---

[33] Quoted in Frame, *The Doctrine of the Christian Life*, 247.

[34] Ibid.

[35] Ibid., 245.

[36] VanDrunen, *Living in God's Two Kingdoms*, 193. he does say there is a unique Christian subjective perspective on work, 191.7

[37] Frame, *The Doctrine of the Christian Life*, 244.

C. The Redemptive Kingdom

To conclude this chapter, I want to briefly look at the emphasis on the local church gathering in R2K thought. A consideration of the redemptive kingdom will bring us naturally to Part 3, chapter 7, where we will consider the role of the local church in the life of the believer and in God's purposes in this world. This section will, accordingly, be briefer than what has preceded it. If family life, vocation, politics, and non-religious activity are features of the common kingdom, then all that remains for the redemptive kingdom is the gathering of the local church. This is something that VanDrunen is explicit about. Christians live subjectively in the common kingdom according to faith but live according to the natural law that God has ordained to govern that kingdom.[38] The local church gathered is where the commands of Scripture and God's redemptive purposes are accomplished: "Participation in the life of the church, not participation in cultural activities of the broader world, is central for the Christian life."[39] This contrasts strongly with the transformationalist position: for the transformationalist, all of life lived out of faith in Jesus Christ is redemptive. In this sense, the church describes not only God's people gathered but also these same people working out their faith day-to-day. I find VanDrunen's emphasis on the local church refreshing in light of views, including some held by transformationalists, that see the Church universal (all Christians regardless of their local gatherings) and the daily labours in the world to be as significant or more significant than the local church. However, I think VanDrunen's contention that the New Testaments focuses on the local church *gathered* is mistaken. He contrasts his view with those that characterize the local church as a "gas station" where we get filled up for the real work of the Christian life throughout the week.[40] This is the language and thought of some groups, yet this is an extreme. It would be wrong to go to the other extreme and say that the gathered church is what the New Testament focuses on. The focus on the local church makes sense in the context of the two kingdoms teaching, yet its exegetical foundation is wanting.

---

[38] VanDrunen, *Living in God's Two Kingdoms*, 187–194.

[39] Ibid., quote from page 133; see all of chapter 6.

[40] VanDrunen, *Living in God's Two Kingdoms*, 132.

VanDrunen appeals to many texts to show the significance of the local church: this includes it being the focus of corporate worship, the preaching and teaching of the word, and the Lord's supper.[41] I would not want to diminish this: the gathering of the local church ought to be held in far higher esteem than most of us have held it.[42] Corporate worship is indeed a special time in the life of Christian and prefigures eternity that awaits us. The Lord's supper is specially reserved for the gathered church, and the teaching ministry of the church is especially expressed when it is gathered. However, the New Testament does not restrict the life of the church to the gathered church alone. This will be the topic of the next chapter, but to prefigure this point, consider one line of argument with me.

After identifying the local church gathered as the focus of the redemptive kingdom, VanDrunen then outlines the distinctive ethic of the church in contrast with the world. However, it seems that he intends this ethic to be practice only within the context of the church gathered,[43] which does not fit with the New Testament's portrait of the church nor its ethic. If we consider the "church" on a purely linguistic basis, the New Testament uses the term (ἐκκλησία, *ekklesia*, "church")[44] to refer to the local groups of believers without reference to their gathering (e.g. Acts 8:1, 11:22, 26; 14:23; Rom 16:1; 1 Cor 1:2), to these groups gathered (e.g. Matt 18:17; 1 Cor 11:18; 1 Cor 14:19, 28), and to the total of all believers throughout the world (e.g. Matt 16:18; Acts 5:11, 8:3; 1 Cor 10:32). If one wants to use the term

---

[41] Ibid., 134–136.

[42] As I write this (May, 2020) we are in the midst of the Covid-19 related lockdown in New South Wales, Australia. I think many of us in the Western world are feeling a newfound appreciation for the local church gathered in a time when it is not permitted.

[43] After emphasizing the unique focus on the church as a gathered worshipping community, it would seem that his repeated references to this ethic as the church's unique redemptive ethic and his argument from the keys locate the whole life of the church in its gathering. "Believers and groups of believers do not constitute 'the church' in everything they do" (117). VanDrunen, *Living in God's Two Kingdoms*, 100–117. Cf. David VanDrunen, "Bearing Sword in the state, Turning Cheek in the Church: A Reformed Two-Kingdoms Interpretation of Matthew 5:38–42," *Themelios* 34, no. 3 (2009).

[44] In other contexts, this term is used primarily with the sense "gathering," so it is significant that a prominent NT use of the word is *not* for a literal gathering.

"church" solely for the gathered church, I would have no objection; it must only be made clear that this is not the only way the Bible uses the word. It should be clear from the few references cited here that the Bible conceives of Christians as local groups and a universal body regardless of whether they gather or not.[45] Most of the biblical instructions in the New Testament regard the church as it functions outside of the gathered context (e.g. Ephesians 5, Colossians 3, Philemon). Particularly instructive are the gift lists in Romans 12:3-8, 1 Corinthians 12:11-31, and Ephesians 4:1-16. Though many of these gifts have an expression in the local gathering, most cannot be restricted to these gatherings. Teaching, evangelism, and prophecy happen within the gathered church but are never restricted to the gathering. Tongues with an interpretation can occur within the gathered church, but it apparently is intended for private practice (1 Corinthians 14). Surely God does not only heal in the gathered church. Yet these gifts are given for the building up of the body of Christ so that it might function as God intended it; if these gifts are used outside of the gathered context, then it is hard to see how we can restrict the "church" or the "redemptive kingdom" to the gathered body—if we intend with "redemptive kingdom" God's specific purpose for creating the people of God and spreading Christ's kingdom. Indeed, evangelism involves going out beyond the boundaries of the gathering to make the Gospel known (Rom 10:5-21). The Sermon on the Mount, the kingdom ethic *par excellence* cannot be restricted to the gathered church alone; how else will we be salt and will the world give glory to God because of our good works (Matt 5:13-16)? The point is this: if the majority of the work associated with God's people and the spreading of the kingdom happens outside of the gathered church—indeed, if there are particular behaviours that ought to characterize Christian families (a "common kingdom" institution), behaviours that are meant to image the church's relationship with Christ—it is hard to see how we can make any meaningful distinction between the "common" and "redemptive" kingdom. It is more meaningful to make a distinction between the believer and the unbeliever and to emphasize the

---

[45] In a recent book, *One Assembly,* Jonathan Leeman argues that by definition a "church" is a gathering. In my review, I deal with some of the lexical evidence and identify the problems in his argument. Jonathan Leeman, *One Assembly: Rethinking the Multisite and Multiservice Church Models,* 9marks (Wheaton, Illinois: Crossway, 2020); J. Alexander Rutherford, "Review of One Assembly," *Teleioteti,* May 25, 2020, accessed June 7, 2020, https://teleioteti.ca/2020/05/25/review-of-one-assembly/.

importance of the gathering of God's people in the regular rhythm of faithful Christian, or kingdom, living.

It is to this we will now turn; in Part 3, we will consider the biblical teaching on Christian cultural engagement form three perspectives, ecclesiology, soteriology, and eschatology. Our discussion of ecclesiology, the nature of the church, will be a natural extension of our discussion here.

PART 3—

Loving the West Enough to Watch It Burn

ECCLESIOLOGY: FUNDAMENTAL ALLEGIANCE

> And let us not grow weary of doing good, for in due season we will reap, if we do not give up. So then, as we have opportunity, let us do good to everyone, and especially to those who are of the household of faith. – Galatians 9:9-10

In the last two parts, we considered the value of "saving the West" through the lens of history—how Christians supposedly saved the West in the past—and theological ethics, how Christians think we should act towards and save the West today. We concluded that the two significant positions on Christian cultural engagement were incompatible with the Bible and that the whole endeavour to save the West is misguided. Our goal is not to save Western Culture. In doing so, we briefly saw our true purpose on Earth, to make disciples and teach them obedience in the context of a local church so that the lost would be saved and those who are in Christ would come to know and love him with all their heart, soul, mind, and strength. In the following three chapters, I want us to consider this purpose—God's purpose for Christians and his Church—under three headings, ecclesiology, soteriology, and eschatology. In doing so, we will see that we are called to change the world, but this change is far more drastic and far different than it is usually presented. In the words of Peter,

> The Lord is not slow to fulfill his promise as some count slowness,

> but is patient toward you, not wishing that any should perish, but that all should reach repentance. But the day of the Lord will come like a thief, and then the heavens will pass away with a roar, and the heavenly bodies will be burned up and dissolved, and the earth and the works that are done on it will be exposed.
>
> Since all these things are thus to be dissolved, what sort of people ought you to be in lives of holiness and godliness, waiting for and hastening the coming of the day of God, because of which the heavens will be set on fire and dissolved, and the heavenly bodies will melt as they burn! But according to his promise we are waiting for new heavens and a new earth in which righteousness dwells. (2 Pet 3:9-13)

It is not that we should not save the West; it is that the West, the entire world, needs a change far more drastic than we could accomplish. Every citizen of Satan's kingdom is on a one-way train to Hell, the second death—eternal torment under the wrath of God coming forth from his throne. The institutions of our world are raised in and shaped by opposition to God and his King, Jesus Christ. The entire creation, Paul tells us in Romans 8, has been cursed by God and is subject to futility, longing for the day God would remove his curse. The West, our world, desperately needs change; the citizens of darkness need to see and savour the light; the futility of creation needs to be undone and restored to God's good purpose for it. These are things that no amount of common kingdom or transformational labours can accomplish. God has revealed how he will accomplish this change, by obliterating the old creation and creating a new heaven and new earth "in which righteousness dwells" (2 Pet 3:13). Yet we have a place in this change God is working, in the new creation he is making. In Peter's terms, we are to wait for and hasten this day of God, the day of his vengeance against all sin and rebellion. For Peter, this "hastening" is accomplished by living lives of "holiness," that is, lives fully dedicated to God's purpose, and of Godliness, lives fully shaped in the imitation of God's character (2 Pet 3:11).

As we saw in the Introduction, G.K. Chesterton charged the Greek Stoic philosophers—who thought so much about ethics and the nature of society—with the failure to do and desire to do what was necessary to actually see change implemented. When faced with something needing change, two errors present themselves in seeking change. On the one hand, it is possible to recognize the world's faults and yet love it too much to risk changing those faults. On the other hand, it is possible to not love the world enough to put in the effort to change it. The person who brings change is the one who loves the world enough to watch it burn. Too often we Christians are guilty of the charge that we "do not love the city enough to set fire to it."[1]

To what extent are we willing to go to see true change, to see the lost saved, to see Christ return and the new creation inaugurated? Are we willing to give up our comforts, are we willing to give up our money, our time, future opportunities for our children, in order that change might happen? I remember one conversation I had with a close friend of mine; he was honest with me; he could not imagine what it would be like to live under an Islamic state or West dominated by the Left. Such a world would be terrible for raising our kids. But what if these were the means that God would use to save this world? What if the world needs to get worse before it gets better? What if the West needs to burn before it can be saved? Are we willing to give up the comforts and freedoms afforded us in this society if it means God's kingdoms come and his will be done?

On the other hand, maybe we hate this world too much. This is the attitude of those who are "so heavenly minded that they are of no earthly good," as the old saying goes. If we are so focused on "getting into heaven," whether we are deceived by works-righteousness or so focused on enduring in the faith and ensuring our family endures that we neglect our broader Christian responsibilities, we show that we really do not love this world enough to do what God has called us to.

Now, do not get me wrong; I am not calling for Christians to literally burn their cities or their countries to the ground. Nor am I calling for Christians to transform the culture into a Christendom. Instead, we will see that the Bible calls us to live in such a way that puts to shame the structures and ways of life of our world, that unveils their inconsistencies and demonstrates that the only true hope in this world is Christ. The world will burn when Christ comes to judge it; our job is not to stop that future but to "hasten the coming of our Lord" (2 Pet 3:12). We need to love the people of the West enough to watch Western society fall apart. We need to love the lands, animals, and creative potential of humanity living in those lands enough to long for the day when the curse will be rolled back, the present

---

[1] Chesterton, *Orthodoxy*, 69.

world dissolved as with fire, and a new, perfect, sinless, and peaceful creation erected in its place (2 Pet 3:11-13). I think that if we live consistently the way the Bible calls us to live, things will change. At times, change will bring benefits to those outside the Church, as we say in Part 1, but this cannot be our goal or expectation. In this Part, Chapters 7-9, we are going to look at three different biblical perspectives by which we can view the Christian life. All of these look at the expression of the kingdom mandate Jesus gave his people in Matthew 28:18-20 (the great commission) in the life of the Church, encompassing and showing us our role as individuals within the Church. Because the Church is the expression of Christ's heavenly rule on earth, it is often called the Kingdom of God or of Heaven.

It should now be clear that by rejecting the Reformed Two Kingdoms view of the "Redemptive Kingdom" in the last chapter, I do not want to suggest that a "Redemptive Kingdom" is not a concept in Scripture or a helpful way of looking at the Christian life. Instead, I only hoped to show that this kingdom can not be easily partitioned from the rest of human life nor restricted to the gathered church. Christ has established a kingdom, yet this kingdom extends throughout the globe, touches on every aspect of a Christians life, and is in conflict with the hostile kingdom that dominates this world. In this and the following two chapters, I want to look at the biblical teaching about the Christian life from three different perspectives, or through three different theological lenses. I will employ several New Testament pictures to describe the nature of the Church, but the primary pictures found in Scripture is that of "kingdom," which we will consider in Chapter 8. The Church, referring to God's people, make up his kingdom, the sphere and expression of his kingdom; we will look at the Church in this chapter. A third picture is that of the "new creation": Christians are new creations, foretastes of the coming new heaven and new earth; we will look at Christians as new creations, and so strangers or exiles in the Old Creation, in Chapter 9.

Our plan for this chapter will be simple: first, we will consider the nature of the Church in the New Testament and some broader implications for the way we think about the Christian life. Second, we will focus on the local church and consider its nature and function when gathered and when dispersed throughout the week.

A. The Church

There are several ways we can and often do think of our relationships to one another, both what unites us and demarcates us from others. "Identity" is a key concept in our culture, capturing the essential social category or categories through which we perceive ourselves. For Christians, we receive our primary identity through God's gracious election and his gift of salvation. We are primarily those who follow Christ, who are identified with him and acknowledge him as our Lord and Saviour: we are Christians.

Because our society often finds identity in self-identification, in how we choose to believe and present ourselves, identity is often void of responsibility. However, there are cases where identity involves responsibility and obligation; to be "Canadian" means I bear some relation to that nation, often the legal relationship of citizenship. To be Canadian, then, means I have certain responsibilities towards that government. I may also feel the social responsibility to represent "Canadians" in a positive light. To be a "parent" means I have certain obligations towards a dependant, a child. Christian identity is often treated as the non-obligatory sort; it is often treated as the self-adopted sort of identity, like "gamer," "conservative," or "bookworm." However, the Bible does not treat Christian identity in this way: to be a "Christian" involves fundamental allegiance to Jesus Christ and identification with a certain group of people and with Jesus Christ, who is ruling at the right hand of God the Father and present with his people through the Holy Spirit. To be a Christian is to be fundamentally aligned with Christ's purposes over against all other purposes, or at least to be seeking that goal however imperfectly. To be a Christian is to be fundamentally aligned with Christ's kingdom as it is expressed on earth in the Church. The Church in the Bible is not a building nor even a group of people that get together occasionally; the Church is the fundamental organizational allegiance of the Christian and their primary social identity. In the first regard, the local church is the focus of the entire Christian life; in the second, the Church universal is (or ought to be) more important to the Christian than any other identity marker.

In theological discussion, there are generally three ways that we use the term "church." Each of these corresponds to the way the Bible uses the word ἐκκλησία (*ekklēsia*) to refer to God's New Testament people. A fourth way we use the word "church" in English, to refer to a building, is not found in the Bible. The Greek word itself generally means a gathering or assembly of people, yet it is used in a broader more technical sense in both the New and Old Testament to refer to God's people, whether or not they are gathered. In the first sense, it refers to God's people gathered on "the Lord's day" to fellowship, praise the Lord, and sit under his Word (1 Cor 14:19, 28). In the second sense, it refers to a local group of God's people (e.g. Acts 8:1, 11:22, 26; 14:23; Rom 16:1; 1 Cor 1:2). In the third sense, it refers to all of God's people spread throughout the world (Matt 16:18; Acts 5:11, 8:3; 1 Cor 10:32).[2] It is important to recognize all these senses of "church," which are echoed in the similar term "kingdom," if we are to make sense of the Bible's teaching. There is important continuity between all these senses. The most frequent use of the term is for the local groups of Christians, yet this is often associated with the universal definition; these local groups are "the Church in" some location. They are a part of the universal Church localized in a concrete place. The use of the word "church" for a gathering is the most natural sense of the word, an "assembly," yet the translation "church" is correct, for the significance of such a gathering is that it is God's people, the Church, in a local area gathered together.

The recognition that every local body is united as Christ's body, the universal Church, is important for shaping our interaction with Christians outside our local body. Because we are all part of one church, one group over against all the other groups that characterize this world (false religions, states, ethnicities), we have a unity that transcends our differences. Complete strangers, for this reason, become "brothers and sisters," and hospitality towards such strangers is an essential component of local church life (cf. 2 & 3 John). Because of their unity, Paul can rally the local churches throughout the known world to meet the needs of the church in Jerusalem (1 Cor 16:1-4). The universal Church is an important category, for it makes clear that all of God's people regardless of location, identity markers, or denominational affiliation are united in their mission to make Christ known and disciple his followers. This category helps us think through our obligations as local churches to work with other local churches and help local churches elsewhere in the world. The universal Church is also important for how we as Christians

---

[2] Throughout this book I follow the relatively common practice of capitalizing the word "Church" when referring to the Church universal, all of God's people.

shape our identity over against the world and make decisions. This will be the topic of the following chapter. To prefigure that conversation, we can observe that in the New Testament, the Church provides the essential relation for all human partnership: Christians are not to unite their purposes with anyone who is not part of the universal Church.

That, however, is the topic for the following chapter. The church local is the primary focus of the New Testament, the recipients of its letters and the place where Christ's commission is performed. We could define "church" in this sense as a local, physically demarcated group of Christians with a recognized authority. That is, a local church in the biblical sense is found in one location, has defined boundaries (such that there are certain people who meet as a certain church), and is overseen by an elder/pastor or (ideally) elders/pastors.[3] We will consider now the local church as it is gathered and as it is dispersed.

B. The Gathered Church

David VanDrunen is absolutely right when he grants fundamental importance to the gathered church. The author of Hebrews makes it clear that the local church gathering is of great importance, warning his audience not to neglect "to meet together" in order that they might be encouraged and persevere in their faith (Heb 10:25). He is also right in observing that the metaphor that the gathered church is a "gas station," serving the purpose of refuelling Christians for the work that really matters, 9-5 life, is crass. However, to whatever extent this metaphor is misguided, there remains an element of truth in it. The gathering of the church is important: only there is a whole local church able to gather as one. If a local church is by nature a demarcated body, the gathered church serves this fundamental role of identifying who is part of a specific local church.

---

[3] In many denominations, "pastor" or "minister" are the primary terms for local church leadership, an elder being a lay or administrative leader. However, I believe the biblical language focuses on "elder" with the other terms specifying different roles elders take in the local church. I will use the term "elder" in what follows for the main leadership of the local church. Cf. Acts 14:23; 1 Tim 3:1-7:, 5:17-25; Titus 1:5-9; 1 Pet 5:1-11.

It is only in this context that we partake of the Lord's Supper, God's ordained means for reinforcing that unity and for refreshing our souls with an "enacted promise," with the precious reminder of God's promises fulfilled in and given to us through Christ Jesus.[4] The gathered church in worship is also the place where God's people can be found together praising God, a precious foretaste of eternity where the universal Church will be gathered together in such worship.[5] Finally, the local church gathered is a primary place where the teaching authority of the local church leadership is expressed. I say "a primary" because as protestants we do not believe elders preach from the pulpit *ex-cathedra*, as if here and only here they carry God's authority to address our needs and rebuke us with the Word. Paul commands Timothy and Titus to proclaim the truth of the Gospel, to apply it in exhortation and rebuke, to ensure the Word is read publicly, and to teach the Word (e.g. 1 Tim 4:13, 2 Tim 4:1-5). The public reading of the Scriptures happens primarily in the local church, as the Old Testament Scriptures and the New Testament letters when they were first received were read in the local church (Col 4:16). For these reasons, the local church gathered is of utmost importance. However, it should be observed that many of these functions of the local church have an outward focus: they shape the life of the Christian and equip them in order that they might "fulfill the work of ministry," as Paul puts it in Ephesians 4:11-16. This is something that cannot and does not happen only in the context of the local church gathered. The local church gathered defines a body of baptized believers with a shared mission, overseen by shared leadership, who live out the great commission in their everyday life. The local church demarcated by the gathering is the primary but not sole focus of this ministry.

---

[4] I have found Tim Chester's discussion of the Lord's Supper and Baptism as "enacted promises" quite edifying, though I disagree with several significant points of interpretation in the book. Tim Chester, *Truth We Can Touch: How Baptism and Communion Shape Our Lives* (Wheaton, Illinois: Crossway, 2020); Rutherford J. Alexander, "Review of Truth We Can Touch," *Teleioteti*, April 27, 2020, accessed May 13, 2020, https://teleioteti.ca/2020/04/27/review-of-truth-we-can-touch/.

[5] VanDrunen makes this point in VanDrunen, *Living in God's Two Kingdoms*.

C. The Church Dispersed

In the context of Ephesians 4:11-16, "the work of ministry" is the "building up of the body Christ" (12). The goal is the "unity of faith" and "knowledge of the Son of God" and "mature manhood" for all Christians (13). This corresponds to the second half of the great commission, "teaching them to observe all that I have commanded you" (Matt 28:20). We might be surprised to see how much of the New Testament is focused on this aspect of "ministry," what we could call the internal work or purpose of the local church. The local church is inward-focused: believers work together under the authority and teaching of recognized leaders[6] in order that everyone in the local church might be united and persevere to the end. The latter theme is emphasised in Hebrews 10:25, where the author exhorts his audience that they must not neglect to gather together in order to encourage one another. In the context of Hebrews, this "encouraging" is for the purpose of endurance in faith. What I have called an inward purpose is clear elsewhere in Scripture: in Galatians 6:10, Paul exhorts the Galatians to "do good to everyone, and especially to those who are of the household of faith." In Matthew 5, Jesus commands his followers to be present in the world and a light to it, yet in verse 14 it is clear that he envisages this as a corporate endeavour, "a city on a hill cannot be hidden."[7] The gathered church represents a context where this purpose is fulfilled, yet it is not the only or main context. In their day-to-day life, believers in concrete, local churches are called to fulfil this inward purpose through encouragement, discipleship, and even teaching (though not in the same sense as the teaching performed by recognized leaders). This happens in the vocational setting, as believing bosses treat their believing servants well, and in marriage and family, as

---

[6] I emphasize here and above "recognized" to push against the idea of a self-ordained leader. The pattern in the New Testament is of elders appointing elders. The apostles appointed the first elders and then commissioned these elders to appoint elders in the future (Titus 1:5). The leaders of the church must, therefore, be accredited by other accredited Church leaders.

[7] City is a frequent picture in Scripture, it focuses on two aspects of human life, organization and community. The city of Babylon represents humanity society, community and organization, shaped in opposition to God; the city of Jerusalem represents redeemed society shaped by God's purpose and calling. Cf. Alexander, *The City of God and the Goal of Creation*; Rutherford, "Review of The City of God and the Goal of Creation."

believing spouses and parents lead and encourage one another, and their kids, in the way of the Lord (Eph 5:21-6:9, Col 3:18-4:1, 1 Pet 2:13-3:1-7). As Christians meet in one another's houses, share a coffee, message one another, or do anything for the purpose of building one another up in Christ, they are fulfilling this inward purpose (e.g. Eph 4:17-6:9, Rom 12:1-15:7). Most of the "gifts" given by the Holy Spirit have this purpose (cf. Rom 12:1-3, 1 Cor 12:1- Eph 4:1-11). This inward purpose is also repeatedly identified in the New Testament as care for the impoverished and needy within the local church (e.g. Acts 2:45, 1 Cor 16:1-4, 1 Tim 5:3-16). This purpose is essential to the life of the local church; it is fulfilled both in the church gathered and in the church dispersed. However, the local church does not only have an inward purpose; it also has an outward purpose. Before the command to teach, Jesus commands his disciples to go "and make disciples of all nations, baptizing them in the name of the Father and of the Son and of the Holy Spirit" (Matt 28:19).

This is the local church's outward focus; it is not enough to mature disciples, churches must also multiply themselves through the proclamation of the good news of Jesus Christ's life, death and resurrection—also known as evangelism. It is conceivable that this may happen through the church gathered, such as when an unbeliever comes to a Christmas service or when someone moves from false to true faith. The very act of gathering may also invite attention and lead to salvation. However, far more often, this outward purpose is fulfilled through the church dispersed. The Bible speaks about direct evangelism regularly: people will only come to believe in Jesus if they hear the good news. Unbelievers do not often enter the local church gathering, so it is necessary for the local church to go out to them. It is necessary for its members and leaders to bring the Gospel to their neighbours and co-workers. This is evident in Jesus' own ministry, in the book of Acts, and in passages like Romans 10:13-21. However, a church's outward focus does not end here. In addition to direct evangelism, Paul commends the Galatians to do good "to everyone": "especially to those who are of the household of faith" implies unbelievers are included though not the focus of "everyone" (Gal 6:10). This may justify what some churches call "mercy ministry," general giving and care shown to the needy outside of the local church body. However, the focus is on individual believers doing good in their daily lives: the focus is on the church dispersed.

In addition to "doing good," the New Testament also calls believers to live in a distinct way before unbelievers in order that "they may see your good works and give glory to your Father who is in heaven" (Matt 5:16). This is echoed by Peter, "Keep your conduct among the Gentiles honorable, so that when they speak against you as evildoers, they may see your good deeds and glorify God on the day of visitation" (1 Pet 2:12; cf. Rom 12:14-21,[8] 2 Cor 8:21, Phil 2:15). So, the local church through its individual members performs an outward purpose: it evangelizes, does good, and shines forth the light of Christ in a dark world. The goal of this outward purpose is never to Christianise the world; it is always to see God deliver unbelievers "from the domain of darkness and transfer [them] to the kingdom of his beloved Son" (Col 1:13), to become baptized members of the local church, being taught and teaching others. Throughout the New Testament, this is the primary focus of the Christian life. The Christian life involves allegiance to Christ expressed through identity with and allegiance to his kingdom manifest through a local church. We have already seen that the purpose of the local church, inward and outward, saturates the Christian life; in every area, family and vocation, friendship and even enmity, Christians are to seek to fulfil God's purpose in community with and under the authority of a specific local church. In closing, I want to consider two ways this local allegiance shapes our lives, beyond the explicit pursuit of these purposes in the ways sketched above. We will then end on some practical implications of our fundamental allegiance to Christ through the local church.

First, if our lives are centred on God's purposes through a local church, how does our work—the ways we labour to make a living—fit into our lives? We cannot say with the transformationalists that our work brings about God's kingdom directly, nor can we follow the R2K folk in seeing our work as intrinsically important because of its common kingdom role. In one sense, we can affirm the indirect value of such labour because it brings us into contact with the world, a necessary condition for reaching it. However, the Bible says more than this. Consider Ephesians 4:28, "The one who steals must steal no longer; rather he must labour, doing good with his own hands,

---

[8] I am focusing in this book on the local church's positive role, but Rom 12:20-21 highlights a negative function. As individual believers and the local church live out the Gospel in daily life, it will harden the hearts of some unbelievers and lead to further judgment. This is the church's "negative" role, to push rebels further into their rebellion and so prefigure God's final judgment.

so that he may have something to share with the one who has need." Why does Paul say the thief ought to stop stealing? He does not appeal to the Ten Commandments, though this would be valid enough; instead, he shows the positive role that a Christians labour should perform. Thievery is bad, in this context, because it does not allow for generosity; in its place, the thief ought to work hard "that he may have something to share with the one who has need." The local church needs resources to function, to pay its elders (e.g. 1 Tim 5:17-18) and to take care of those in its congregation who have needs (e.g. 1 Tim 5:3-8). Work is good and necessary, Paul says, because it contributes to those in need. This is echoed by other passages that warn against idleness, lest the church be impoverished and be unable to perform its inward purpose or its members find in idleness the temptation to spiritual vice (1 Thess 4:9-12; 2 Thess 3:6-12; 1 Tim 5:16). So, work also has the important function of providing for the church's ministry and providing for one's own family so that the church can take care of those who are truly in need (cf. 1 Tim 5:8).

Therefore, in the Christian life, work takes on a church-oriented focus. The church also replaces extended and even immediate family as our closest relationships. This overlaps with our next chapter, so I will not go to depth here. But Jesus, when told that his mother and brothers wanted to speak with him, responded by pointing to his disciples, those who followed him and did the will of God, and identifying them as his true family (Mark 3:31-35). This is not only the case for Jesus; it is also true of his disciples. He warns his followers that following him would often mean being hated and despised—even betrayed—by their closest family (Matt 10:21-22; Mark 13:12; Luke 14:26). After telling the rich young man to sell everything and follow him, Peter asks what will happen for Jesus' disciples, who have given everything to follow him. Jesus responds, after commenting on the specific reward awaiting the twelve apostles, "everyone who has left houses or brothers or sisters or father or mother or children or lands, for my name's sake, will receive a hundredfold and will inherit eternal life" (Matt 19:29). In Mark's account (Mark 10:29-30), Jesus emphasizes that this hundredfold reward is realized in this life. It is not found in physical prosperity, for Jesus promises his disciples hardship and persecution; instead, it is realized in the local church and the universal Church. In the local church, we find immediate family; in the universal Church, we find an extended family that stretches across the globe. In the next chapter, we will see that this allegiance has significant implications for our lives.

For now, I want to conclude with one observation and practical application that pertains to the local church. If the local church, as I have argued, is the centre of Christ's purpose working out on earth, how should our lives be shaped by that purpose? For one, that the local church is more immediately important than the universal Church means we should strive for a permanent, long-term commitment in a single local church. Only in such a context will the inward purpose be fully realized, only when Christ's people grow together in committed, long-term, and trusting relationships. In this context, brothers and sisters can care for one another and the elders over a congregation can develop the insight and trust necessary to speak the truth to the needs of the sheep. This means that local church involvement should take priority over success in the workplace. If the primary purpose of work is to serve the purpose of the local church, then allegiance to the local church should have an essential role in the choice of where and when to work. If the commitment to a job would deprive someone of the opportunity to be fully part of the local church life, including its important weekly gatherings, then the priority ought to fall on the local church. If a promotion requires moving away from the church to which one is committed, or if a workplace demands such a move, our commitment to the local church ought to guide our decisions in this matter.

Now, in stressing commitment to the local church, we should be clear that the local church to which we ought to commit *may not be the church we grew up in*. That is, as we acquire the skills necessary to "labour with our hands," we may have to move around a bit (I have lived in four cities over the last eleven years); however, our goal in all our decision making should be to be in a position as soon as is wise for long term commitment to a specific congregation. If a local church is not a given in your situation, finding a church should be done prayerfully. A good place to start is looking where you live; if the church is intended to be the centre of our earthly lives, we ought to seek to be in a position to participate regularly in its gatherings and be in close proximity to others who are part of it. Often, in the Western world, there will be many churches in a single area, so you should find a local church that preaches the Gospel faithfully and is grounded in solid theology. Unfortunately, I do not have space here to provide a full outline of things to look for, but I have provided two resources in the footnotes that go a bit further than I have here.⁹

In this chapter we have considered how ecclesiology, or the doctrine of the Church, shapes the Christian life. The local church is the focus of the Christian life: we can speak of the role of the church as that of our fundamental allegiance; it ought to take priority in our planning and thinking. Our work does not directly transform the world, but it provides the resources and opportunities for the church to fulfil its purpose. The family, the workplace, and every other area of life outside the church gathering are not a "common kingdom" separated from the local church and its life but spheres within which the outward and inward purposes of the church are fulfilled. In the following chapter, we will turn to the universal Church and consider the way our identity as part of Christ's body extended throughout the earth shapes our actions and our engagement with unbelievers and institutions that are not the local church.

---

⁹ "How Do I Find a Good Church?," *Desiring God*, last modified February 7, 2020, accessed May 14, 2020, https://www.desiringgod.org/interviews/how-do-i-find-a-good-church; "What Should I Look for in a Church?," *9Marks*, accessed May 14, 2020, https://www.9marks.org/answer/what-should-i-look-church/.

8

SOTERIOLOGY: REDEMPTIVE INSURGENCY

> Do not be unequally yoked with unbelievers. For what partnership has righteousness with lawlessness? Or what fellowship has light with darkness? What accord has Christ with Belial? Or what portion does a believer share with an unbeliever? What agreement has the temple of God with idols? – 2 Corinthians 6:14-16

In Chapter 7, we saw that the Church becomes the defining identity of the Christian. Our unity with Christ, as part of his body, unites us with believers throughout the world. This unity transcends blood relations, political and ideological positions, citizenship, race, sex, or socioeconomic status. As Paul puts it, "For as many of you as were baptized into Christ have put on Christ. [28]There is neither Jew nor Greek, there is neither slave nor free, there is no male and female, for you are all one in Christ Jesus" (Rom 3:27-28). This has important implications for how we relate to one another. However, his fundamental identity does not only unite; it also demarcates a significant division among humanity. Describing his ministry, Jesus told his disciples,

> Do not think that I have come to bring peace to the earth. I have not come to bring peace, but a sword. For I have come to set a man against his father, and a daughter against her mother, and a daughter-in-law against her mother-in-law. And a person's enemies will be those of his own household. Whoever loves father or

mother more than me is not worthy of me, and whoever loves son or daughter more than me is not worthy of me. And whoever does not take his cross and follow me is not worthy of me. Whoever finds his life will lose it, and whoever loses his life for my sake will find it. (Matt 10:34-39)

To identify ourselves with Jesus is to identify ourselves with God over against the Devil and all humanity who follow in his rebellion. As we saw in Chapter 5, there is a conflict in this created order, a war on a cosmic scale. On the one hand, there is the kingdom of Satan over fallen humanity; on the other, there is the kingdom of Jesus Christ, breaking into the territory ruled by Satan and reclaiming it for the glory of God. If humanity is fundamentally identified with Satan and so opposed to God, it makes sense why they would hate us—those who represent their enemy. If we are acting as the Church, we will be hated:

If the world hates you, know that it has hated me before it hated you. If you were of the world, the world would love you as its own; but because you are not of the world, but I chose you out of the world, therefore the world hates you. Remember the word that I said to you: 'A servant is not greater than his master.' If they persecuted me, they will also persecute you. If they kept my word, they will also keep yours. (John 15:18-20)

What we see in Scripture, therefore, is an antithesis between two warring kingdoms. We can call this a "redemptive antithesis" because it is at the heart of the Christian doctrine of salvation, or soteriology.

The Gospel is originally introduced in Genesis in these terms: "I will put enmity between you and the woman, and between your offspring and her offspring; he shall bruise your head, and you shall bruise his heel" (Gen 3:15). This theme of the offspring of the woman crushing the head of Serpent and defeating his offspring shows up throughout Scripture in the expectation that the Messiah will subdue his enemies, that he will defeat God's enemies: "Sit at my right hand, until I make your enemies your footstool" (Ps 110:1). The image of enemies crushed beneath the feet is a common biblical image for total subjection (e.g. Josh 10:24), yet in light of Genesis 3:16, it takes on additional symbolic significance. Jesus identifies his own opposition with the Pharisees along these lines, calling them—much to their chagrin—children of Satan: "You are of your father the devil, and your will is to do your father's desires" (John 8:44). And in Romans 16:20, Paul anticipates Jesus' final victory as the day when "The God of peace will soon crush Satan under your feet." This war took a decisive turn with Jesus crucifixion and resurrection: the victory has been guaranteed, yet it is not fully secured. The New Testament describes Jesus ministry, culminating in the crucifixion, as the binding of Satan: he is cast out of heaven, no longer able to accuse God's people (Luke 10:18-20; John 12:31; Rev 12:9); he is bound, no longer able to hold on to the nations he has deceived (Mark 3:27; Rev 20:1-3; cf. John 16:11; Col 2:15). Though horribly wounded, Satan has not been finally crushed. He can still prowl around like a roaring lion (1 Pet 5:8). The book of Revelation portrays this conflict as under God's complete control yet nevertheless a trial for God's people. That victory is secured does not diminish the need for battles to be fought day by day. Christ's kingdom has arrived, but fallen humanity is still ruled by their god, the Devil (2 Cor 4:1-6), the prince of the power of the air (Eph 2:1-2; cf. 6:10-20). There will, therefore, be constant warfare between the seed of the Woman—Christ and his body—and the seed of Satan, all of humanity under the power of sin and death.

In light of this conflict, the Bible portrays our salvation as a transfer of allegiance; we are delivered from the kingdom of darkness into the God's glorious light (Gal 1:4; Col 1:13-14). The implications of this should be obvious by now: the "common kingdom," though sovereignly overseen by God (Rom 13:1-7; cf. Hab 1:5, 3:1-19; Isa 44:26), is nevertheless a kingdom hostile towards God and his people. Our interactions with it must, therefore, be governed by an understanding of distinction, of separation, and of hostility. Anything we do within its institutions, for the general good or specific kingdom purposes, will be by necessity "insurgency," or subterfuge. That is, as we live in the world, we are living in a society that presupposes the rejection of God's rule and its identity with Satan's kingdom; we cannot interact with unbelievers and secular institutions as though they were neutral or as if they play by God's rules.[1] In as much as we can in good conscience do so, we play by their rules to achieve God's purposes. This requires extraordinary wisdom, such as no one of us possesses. However, under the guidance of the Holy Spirit, in submission to Scripture, and with the help of

---

[1] By "secular," I mean all institutions that are not the local church, and more broadly, every human endeavour that is not conducted by Christian's self-consciously pursuing God's purposes in this world.

one another, the situation is not so dire. For the rest of this chapter, I want to examine several key texts that guide us in living within hostile territory for God's purposes. We will begin with the clearest yet far-reaching and challenging biblical teaching concerning our relationships with the unbelieving world. We will then turn and consider three significant ethical issues that are usually dealt with in books such as this, Christians and the state, the appropriate actions to take when someone involved in the state or another secular institution repents, and a general Christian approach to secular education (primary, secondary, or post-secondary). Each of these topics involves gathering and reflecting upon many biblical themes, so we must tread with humility in these matters. I can only offer my careful reflections upon the Bible and these matters.

A. Living in Antithesis

If you grew up in the Western church as I did, you might have experienced dozens of youth group sermons cautioning against romantic relationships with unbelievers. The key text here would be 2 Corinthians 6:14-7:1. This is not a wrong application of the text, one echoed in many reputable works (e.g. VanDrunen's *Living in God's Two Kingdoms*). However, we miss the force of this text if we think of it *only* as a prohibition against romantic relationships with unbelievers.

> Do not be unequally yoked with unbelievers. For what partnership has righteousness with lawlessness? Or what fellowship has light with darkness? What accord has Christ with Belial? Or what portion does a believer share with an unbeliever? What agreement has the temple of God with idols? For we are the temple of the living God; as God said,
>
> > I will make my dwelling among them and walk among them, and I will be their God, and they shall be my people. Therefore go out from their midst, and be separate from them, says the Lord, and touch no unclean thing; then I will welcome you, and I will be a father to you, and you shall be sons and daughters to me, says the Lord Almighty.
>
> Since we have these promises, beloved, let us cleanse ourselves from every defilement of body and spirit, bringing holiness to

completion in the fear of God. (2 Cor 6:14-7:1)

Paul does something fascinating here; he takes the Old Testament concept of physical separation and applies it to the Church in a new manner, in terms of spiritual separation. In the Old Testament, God gives his people a complicated law regulating their everyday behaviour; the point of the laws concerning separation is to symbolize and highlight the distinct nature of Israel over against its neighbours. Many of the instructions establish a clear, physical contrast, such as not eating certain foods or refraining from tattoos and body markings (Lev 19:28). However, others symbolize the physical distinction to which Israel is called, such as the command not to mix fabrics in their clothing or use two different building materials in a home (Lev 11:1-47; 19:19). If Israel were obedient to God's commands, they would enjoy the presence of their God among them (Lev. 26:1-13). As God promised to be with his people in the Old Testament, Paul sees this same promise given and fulfilled for us (2 Cor 7:1, cf. 2 Cor 1:20). The fact that Christians together are the temple of God, that they are the place where his presence is known on earth, means that we ought to "cleanse ourselves from every defilement of body and spirit, bringing holiness to completion in the fear of God" (2 Cor 7:1). We know from Jesus' teaching and Paul's first letter to the Corinthians that this does not mean we ought to withdraw from all relationships and contact with unbelievers; how then would we reach them with the Gospel (John 17:15; 1 Cor 5:9-11)? Therefore, we must ask what sort of separation Paul calls for, what "defilement" he commands Christians to avoid.

In 2 Corinthians 6:14, Paul writes, "Do not be unequally yoked with unbelievers." For many of us who have grown up in the city, the image here may be unfamiliar. A yoke is used to connect two animals together to complete a task through their shared strength. It unites their working potential for a shared purpose. To be unequally yoked, therefore, is to be wrongly paired in a relationship, mismatched. To be unequally yoked is to work together for a purpose with someone that is not aligned with the same purpose or not appropriate for the pairing. Paul then elaborates; "what partnership has righteousness with lawlessness?" (2 Cor 6:14.) What business do followers of Christ have with followers of the Devil, those in rebellion against God (who are "lawless")? The following verses unpack this idea with several contrasts, light with darkness, Christ with Belial (i.e. Satan), believers with unbelievers, or God's temple with idols (vv. 15-16). The point is clear: Christians must not be mismatched with or united in purpose with unbelievers. This certainly applies to marriage, as Paul makes clear in his first letter (1 Cor 7:39). Indeed, Paul's application of this principle to marriage should emphasize how drastic this antithesis is. According to Jesus, it is sinful for a Christian to divorce and remarry, except in the case of adultery (Matt 5:32, 1 Cor 7:10-11). However, Paul clarifies that if an unbelieving spouse leaves a believing spouse, the believing spouse has "peace," they *can* remarry, though only in the Lord (1 Cor 7:12-16, 7:39). In this case, the unbeliever initiates the separation; so long as the unbeliever is willing, the believer is called by Paul to preserve the relationship that God might work salvation for their unbelieving spouse and children. The marriage ought to be upheld because it may be used by God to further His purpose of salvation: but if it is broken by the unbeliever, remarriage is allowed. Allegiance to Christ reconfigures even the closest family relationships; the immediate family will experience division (Matt 10:34-39), and marriages may fracture. This makes sense in light of what we have seen: if unbelieves are fundamentally opposed to Christ in their allegiances and purposes (cf. Rom 1:18ff), then any partnership with an unbeliever will involve a fundamental conflict of purposes. If God's purpose through the local church, to spread his kingdom on earth, is to be the centre of the Christian life, shaping all decision making, then *every endeavour can be endangered by an unequal partnership*. We cannot separate physically from the world, but we must be diligent to be holy in our purposes and the relationships we use to pursue them, completely devoted to Christ. It should be clear that the implications here reach far beyond marriage, and primarily concern *entering relationships* (we will consider Paul's teaching below concerning those already in such relationships). Just as we would not enter into a marriage with an unbeliever, we must be diligent not to enter into any partnership with unbelievers that would cause us to compromise our fundamental allegiance to Christ. This means, I believe, not entering business partnerships, property deals (such as a shared mortgage), or friendships that involve a long term and committed walking together through life with an unbeliever (though, see 1 Cor 5:9-13). More significantly for the sphere of my work (Christian academia), we must not join forces with unbelievers to support the training of Christian ministers. This ought to challenge us in a world where our schools are accredited by secular bodies, supported on certain conditions by Government money, and often use textbooks and even employ teachers of questionable commitment to Christ and orthodox faith.

Someone may retort at this point, if we are to avoid *all* partnerships with the world, how can we avoid physically separating ourselves? Our taxes support the state's purposes; our banking and investments support secular corporations; our groceries and online shopping support secular corporations and monolithic conglomerates. To avoid all partnerships, must we live in complete withdrawal with a completely isolated, self-sustaining economy? This is, of course, preposterous and contradicts the New Testaments clear teaching. However, this is not an inevitable conclusion from what I have argued so far. Several considerations support this. First, the Bible does not present Satan's kingdom as an exact parallel to Christ's. Satan's kingdom is stagnant: it does not have a unifying purpose. Instead, it is humanity under the influence of fallen spirits living in opposition to God. There is no unifying goal here, just a unifying presupposition, namely, hostility to God. Satan will, of course, seek to thwart Christ's kingdom, but Scripture does not present this effort as an organized, purposeful strategy. In contrast, Christ's kingdom is united in a single purpose and functions as an invasion of hostile territory. The concern Paul has in 2 Corinthians 6 is not us joining in on Satan's purposes; instead, he is concerned with us letting partnership with unbelievers thwart God's purpose through us. The relationship is asymmetrical. Paul does not have a problem with Christians supporting the business of idolatry with their meat purchases; his only concern is the corruption of conscience and the undermining of the church (1 Cor 8:1-13; 10:14-22). Similarly, we are encouraged repeatedly to give our taxes to our governments, even though they are extensions of Satan's kingdom (Mark 12:13-17; Rom 13:1-7). Therefore, the concern for us is not how our actions might serve Satan's kingdom but that we do not allow Satan's kingdom to thwart God's purposes through us. So, God's command to us through Paul is not complete withdrawal; instead, as we consider entering relationships, we must prioritize God's purpose and not enter a partnership with unbelievers. I think a significant implication for this spiritual separation is our relationship to the government or the state.

B. Christians and the state

The question of the proper Christian interaction with the state is a massive one. I cannot hope to give a comprehensive account of all the nuances of this discussion; however, I do think there are clear lines of biblical teaching regarding our relationship with the state. The very concept of "state" is not a biblical one, so after exploring the concept and the places it overlaps with Scripture, I then want to argue three biblical theses that ought to govern our decision making as it regards our governments. First, Christians are obligated to obey the state unless it causes a conflict in conscience. Second, Christians cannot and must not attempt to "Christianise" the state. Third, Christians make decisions regarding the state according to conscience and its own (flawed) logic.

The State

An initial difficulty in the discussion of the Christian interaction with "the state" is defining the state. The problem is that what we call the state takes many different forms; the Chinese state is quite different in its scope and actions than the American state, which is itself different from the Canadian or Australian state. Some believe that there is an ideal form of the state, or normative concept of the state, by which we can measure all these different ones. For VanDrunen and Wilson, the ideal state is small; it is the state of capitalism and small government.[2] For many in North American today, the ideal state encourages ideological totalitarianism and institutes a particular agenda at all levels of public life. Though the state on both accounts shares some commonality, such as upholding justice and defending from hostile nations, the scope of its authority is heavily debated. Another level of complexity is introduced when we consider the distribution of authority within a state's governing structure and the manner by which its leaders are chosen. When we turn to the Bible, the picture we get is a complicated one. The only thorough discussion of the state given concerns a unique state, the state or kingdom of Israel. A close examination of the Torah portrays a society with a governing structure that differs vastly from what we consider

---

[2] VanDrunen, *Living in God's Two Kingdoms*, 197–198; Wilson, *Empires of Dirt..*

today to be "the state." The leader is chosen through God's revelation, leading to a divinely mandated dynasty (cf. Deuteronomy 17; 2 Samuel 7). This leader is primarily charged with defensive action and infrastructure management. He leads in submission to the Torah, an extensive law governing every aspect of human life in submission to God. Justice is enacted through appointed judges, the Levitical priesthood, the king, and familial vengeance (Deuteronomy 16-17). Every aspect of society is shaped by allegiance to God and life is structured around a rhythm of work, rest, and worship.

For several reasons, this model of the state cannot be instituted today. For one, it is linked to an explicit covenant that has passed away (cf. Galatians 3, Hebrews 8). Second, it requires an explicit divine mandate which we have not received and, with the closing of the canon, must not expect. Third, God's kingdom is manifest today in a different manner than it was then; all the promises concerning a king and kingdom are fulfilled in Christ, yet he reigns in heaven (e.g. Heb 1:1-5) and his physical kingdom has not yet been instituted (Revelation 21-22). So, when we consider "the state" today, we cannot expect it or act to make it to correspond with this state. God's ideal of a kingdom functioning within the fallen world is not attainable in this age. So, what is left?

Other than the mandate for the kingdom of Israel in the Torah, there is no prescriptive presentation of the state in the Bible. However, we do find the state described. In the Bible, the state is primarily a monarchical society that guards defined borders; it is a kingdom, with a people, king, and defined land. There is usually an explicit connection between the state and religion, with a sanctioned cult. In the New Testament, the Roman government maintains order and justice; from extra-biblical records, we know that Ancient Near Eastern kingdoms functioned in a similar manner (see, for example, *the Code of Hammurabi*). John Frame argues that the state as seen from the perspective of the Bible (both Theocratic Israel and secular nations) evolved out of the basic family structure.[3] We see, for example, a parallel structure in the way that Abraham's family, with its slaves and direct family members, functioned in Genesis 10-21 and the way the nations function elsewhere in Scripture. David VanDrunen argues that the authority of the

---

[3] Frame, *The Doctrine of the Christian Life*, 595–602.

state is a natural evolution of the way God has structured nature.[4] Though there is some descriptive value in both of these observations—that is, they both explain features of past and present nations—they have no normative force. To say that a nation evolved from a basic family structure does not imply that the ideal state should be structured on the model of a family. With one exception, the Bible does not tell us what form or function God has given the state.

That one exception is Romans 13:1-7. Like many other passages in the New Testament (Matt 22:15-22; Mark 12:13-17, Titus 3:1; 1 Pet 2:13), Paul commands Christians to be subject to the governing authorities. Paul tells us that the governing authorities receive their authority from God (cf. John 19:11). They are "God's servants." The focus of their authority here is justice, for punishing the wicked. So, in a sense, the state is commissioned by God for the task of justice. Any authority they possess they have because God has given it to them. When we look at the broader teaching of Scripture—and consider the nature of the government that Paul speaks of, Rome—we are cautioned against thinking too highly of the state in this regard. In the Old Testament, God is clearly sovereign in the rising and falling of the nations around Israel. God orchestrates the rise of the Medo-Persian empire for his purposes, calling Cyrus his "shepherd" and "anointed one" or messiah (Isa 44:28; 45:1). In Habakkuk 1:5, we are told that God had raised up the Babylon empire for a particular purpose. They are his tool for justice, to bring wrath on the unrighteous of Judah. Their king, Nebuchadnezzar is even called his anointed one, or messiah (Hab 3:13).[5] In these contexts, the sword possessed by the state is wielded for justice between nations. So even wicked, pagan nations are God's "servants," and they wield the sword (Rom 13:4) at a national level. But in the context of Romans 13, it would appear that God uses them to employ some semblance of justice—upholding what is right and punishing the wicked—at an individual or civil level (within the nation, 13:3). This gives us a God-given mandate to submit to and trust the state as his

---

[4] VanDrunen, *Living in God's Two Kingdoms*, 153.

[5] See my study guide or commentary on the Book of Habakkuk. J. Alexander Rutherford, *Believe the Unbelievable: A Study in Habakkuk*, Teleioteti Study Guides 1 (Vancouver, BC: Teleioteti, 2018); J. Alexander Rutherford, *The Book of Habakkuk: An Exegetical-Theological Commentary on the Hebrew Text*, A Teleioteti Old Testament Commentary 1 (Vancouver, BC: Teleioteti, 2019).

instrument. However, the passage does not go to a great depth telling us how a state should do this; it merely tells us that God uses states for his purposes in maintaining justice. In addition to theocratic Israel and what we learn from Romans 13, there is another consistent picture of the state in the Bible that we need to consider before we summarize the biblical teaching about the non-theocratic state and consider our interaction with it.

The first indications we get of socio-economic and political organization in Scripture is in the book of Genesis. After Cain and his descendants established the first city (Gen 4:17), a picture in the Bible of human community and organization, we read of Noah's descendants gathering at Babel, a city embodying human ambition and rebellion (Gen 11:1-9). Our first picture of socio-political organization in the Bible is associated with the Kingdom of Satan. In the rest of Genesis, we encounter kings and kingdoms without these negative connotations. However, in later Scripture, particularly the prophetic books and Daniel, we again find the association of kingdoms, of the state, with Satan. Just picking a couple of examples from the prophets, we find Egypt and other nations portrayed in the language of a dragon or Serpent, associating them with the Serpent *par excellence* (Isa 27:1, 51:9; Ezek 29:3-5, 32:2; cf. Psalm 74:14). In Daniel's vision of the beasts, it is significant that the four beasts emerge out of the sea. The sea becomes a symbol of rebellion against God as the Scriptures unfold.[6] The beasts represent different kings ruling over different kingdoms (Dan 7:16, 23); they are portrayed as powerful (the image of "horns") and vicious (cf. 7:5), in opposition to God's people (7:21). They will ultimately be defeated by "one like the son of man" (7:13, 22, 26-27). Thus, the Old Testament represents the nations and their kings as instruments of Satan, as rebels against God, and as enemies of his saints.

All this imagery is found again in the book of Revelation, where the beastly kingdom of man is associated explicitly with the Satanic dragon. The different beasts, representing different institutions within the kingdom of Satan, emerge once more from the sea and are explicitly opposed to Christ

---

[6] J. Alexander Rutherford, "Review of From Chaos to Cosmos," *Teleioteti*, December 12, 2018, accessed March 23, 2020, https://teleioteti.ca/2018/12/12/review-of-from-chaos-to-cosmos/.

and his saints.⁷ This makes perfect sense in light of our earlier exposition of the story of Scripture as a cosmic conflict between Satan's kingdom and Christ's. If all humans are offspring of Satan and in rebellion against Christ, it makes sense that the socio-political institutions they create are likewise aligned with Satan over against God and his Christ. Given what we have seen, that the state is commissioned by God and used for his purposes while nevertheless set up in opposition to him and serving Satan, we can now consider our interaction with the state as Christians.⁸

1) Christians are obligated to obey the state unless it causes a conflict in conscience

Though the nations of this world are in rebellion against God, their rebellion is carefully under control. Like Satan, who is bound yet "prowls around like a roaring lion" (Rev 20:2; 1 Pet 5:8), the nations hate God and oppose his people yet are "the servant of God" who "carries out God's wrath on the wrongdoer" (Rom 13:4, cf. Isa 44:28-45:1, Hab 3:13). Because of this dual nature of the state, rebellious yet anointed, our relationship with states will be necessarily complicated. The clear, default principle in Scripture is to submit to and honour governing authorities. We ought to pay taxes, pray for our governing leaders, and submit to their commands (Mark 12:13-17; Rom 13:1-7; 1 Tim 2:1-2; 1 Pet 2:17). We do so because all authority derives from God, so our submission to them is submission to him (Rom 13:1). The exception to this default is when submission to the state would compromise our submission to God. That is, our ultimate allegiance is to God and his church; our submission to the state is derivative from this relationship. Now, caution is necessary: we must be careful that our disobedience is truly for

---

⁷ I have found Alan Johnson and G.K. Beale to be helpful commentators on this wonderful book. I have also found it particularly insightful to listen to the book in a single sitting. For this purpose, I recommend the *Streetlights Audio Bible*, available at www.streetlightsbible.com. Beale, *The Book of Revelation: A Commentary on the Greek Text*; Alan F. Johnson, "Revelation," in *Hebrews - Revelation*, ed. Tremper Longman III and David E. Garland, Rev. ed., The Expositor's Bible Commentary (Grand Rapids: Zondervan, 2006).

⁸ See my commentary on Habakkuk for a closer examination of God's relationship to Babylon, a particularly brutal nation that is a symbol of opposition to God and his people throughout the Bible.

Christ and not only using Christ as a cover for our own disagreements. A case in point was the COVID-19 crisis in 2020, as I was writing this. My wife and I were blessed by the careful and thoughtful, God-fearing response offered by the Sydney Diocese and Moore Theological College. They have been a model of Christian wisdom and submission to God-appointed authorities. Back home, in North America, there were reports of many churches flaunting the lockdown orders from their governments. This was often justified as the government overstepping their bounds or suppressing religion. However, it is clear in each case that the lockdown applies to *all institutions*, not just the church, so it was not a case of religious suppression (at least as of June).[9] In every case of which I know, online meetings are not discouraged. As for the government overstepping their bounds, we have no biblical norm to discern this. Therefore, with no command from God being broken by submitting (we are called to meet regularly, but we regularly allow exceptions for extraordinary circumstances, and there is no biblical prohibition against online gatherings, though far from ideal), we ought to submit to our governing authorities in this matter. I digress, there are clear cases where we must disobey the state out of submission to Christ.

We could enumerate examples endlessly. Obvious ones are cases where church gatherings are forbidden indefinitely or permanently with no extraordinary reason for the prohibition, or when an otherwise reasonable prohibition means that God's purpose for a specific church would be thwarted (such as significant spiritual harm to the congregation with no other means but disobedience to correct it). That is, when it is a clear case of persecution, Christians must resist. Similarly, if evangelism and conversion are forbidden, as in many Middle Eastern countries, Christians must disobey. In addition to the theological argument, namely, that submission to Christ trumps submission to earthly authority, we have the explicit example of the apostles in this regard. Jesus and Paul are models of submission to earthly authorities—despite Jesus' ultimate authority—yet they are willing to disobey where necessary. Jesus submits to his parents, yet he stays in the temple out of allegiance to his Father (Luke 2:41-52). Paul does not object to his trials

---

[9] There have been, since then, cases where certain governments have been uneven in their handling of these issues, but many of these are explicable as the government not seeing the value in religious institutions, not as active opposition to them.

and the order of Roman law, even appealing to its statutes when it served his purposes (Acts 25:11). However, when authorities demanded that the Apostles stop preaching the Gospel, they continually refuse to obey (Act 4:18-20; 5:17-21, 28). Particularly exemplary of the principle we are expanding is Peter's response to the Sanhedrin's command to stop preaching: "We must obey God rather than men" (Acts 5:29). However, in no case in Scripture is such disobedience presented as a denigration of what continue to be God-appointed authorities: disobedience may be necessary, yet our attitude remains one of quietness and honouring "the Emperor" (1 Tim 2:1-7; 1 Pet 2:13-17).

We discern our obligations to God through Scripture. When we are convicted of what we ought not to do or ought to do, we call this conscience. Sometimes our conscience convicts us of things that are not objectively sinful, however, in these cases we ought to follow our conscience until we are convinced from Scripture that this is not sin (1 Cor 8:9-11; Rom 14:1-23). So, as it is commonly phrased, we must act according to conscience, seeking to form our sense of moral obligation according to Scripture. This, I believe, is the rule: unless doing so would violate our conscience, we must submit to our governing authorities. In the cases where we are convicted by conscience, we must be open to the correction of others lest disobedience to the state hampers the purpose of the church or even puts the name of Christ to shame (cf. 1 Pet 2:11-12).

2) Christians cannot and must not reform the state in conformity with Scripture

Of the many implications of what we have seen so far, one is that we cannot and must not seek to make any earthly state into a "Christendom," or Christian kingdom. However, refraining from doing so may be difficult at times. I think we would all agree that cancer is a horrid disease, causing unimaginable pain to those who suffer and their families. Imagine having the cure for cancer yet knowing that releasing it would cause repercussions far more damaging. This is a choice none of us would wish to have. What if we had the answer to a most pressing crisis, yet knew that solving it would cause a crisis of a different sort? Such a conundrum is, I believe, at the heart of the question about Christian reformation of the state. When it comes to reforming the state, Christians face something we could call *the theocratic paradox.*

a. Paradox 1 - The Theocratic Paradox

Our world is infected with a disease as pernicious as cancer. Sin has dug its roots deep into the hearts of men and fallen angels, creating a wicked world-system under the rule of Satan. Sin, playing out in the actions of men and spiritual beings, produces all sorts of twisted and corrupt socio-political systems worldwide. In one sense, Christians have an answer to this disease that we are free to implement; by preaching the good news of the Gospel, we offer freedom from the bondage of sin and its effects. Yet the Bible also offers a different picture; throughout its pages, it presents a picture of an ideal socio-political system, the ideal government for a fallen world. The wisdom of the biblical Law puts to shame every human political invention, yet as Christians we are unable—indeed, prohibited from—implementing this Law on earth. Such is the theocratic paradox, having in our hands the answer to many of our world's problems but unable and prohibited from implementing it. Even though he argues that it is no longer in effect, Paul nevertheless identifies the Torah as a good thing (Rom 7:7-12). How could he not? It was delivered by God himself. It was not a final solution, yet it offers an attractive vision for society.

Ruled by a benevolent, God-fearing ruler (Deuteronomy 17), it would be deliberate in excluding all unbelief, which causes much division and damage in a society (e.g. Deut 12:29-13:18). It makes provision for poverty through short term, indentured slavery and the provisions for gleaning (Deut 15:7-18; Lev 19:9-18), thus solving the double problem of meeting a need while not encouraging sloth and laziness (cf. 2 Thess 3:6-12). Though flawed in many serious ways—including its theological program—Rousas Rushdoony's three-volume *Institutes of the biblical Law* has done the Church a favour by showing the coherence and beauty of the Torah.[10] The rule of law is mediated by judges and the priesthood in submission to the Torah

---

[10] Rushdoony, *The Institutes of biblical Law.* Cf. Waltke and Yu, *An Old Testament Theology;* John M Frame, "The Institutes of biblical Law: A Review Article," *The Works of John Frame and Vern Poythress*, accessed May 17, 2020, https://frame-poythress.org/the-institutes-of-biblical-law-a-review-article/.

(Deut 16:18-17:20), and the personal involvement of wronged parties in the enactment of punishments brings the true consequences of sin into brutal proximity with everyday life (e.g. Num 34:19). A diligent study of the Torah, with attention to its deep symbolism and the nature of its legal provisions, will reward the reader with a profound sense of God's wisdom and justice. However, we are forbidden from enacting this society on earth. For one, it is connected intimately with the Old Covenant, which has passed away (e.g. Galatians 3, Hebrews 8). It is symbolically oriented to the coming of Jesus Christ, so much of what it anticipates symbolically has been fulfilled in reality (such as the sacrificial system, cf. Hebrews 4:14-10:18). It also requires an explicit divine anointing for its king, which has been fulfilled in Christ.[11] That is, since Jesus is currently ruling, there is no place for an earthly king over an earthly kingdom. This is the general contour of the paradox: the ideal state in a fallen world is presented in the Torah, but the progression of redemptive history demonstrates that such a state is unsustainable in this creation; humanity is too mired in sin. We must await a new creation perfected under Christ's rule for society to be perfected. We can zoom in and identify several specific points of paradox within this broader paradox.

b. Paradox 2 – There Is No Way to Distinguish the Application of Different Moral Principles in Scripture

In the process of forming a Christendom, the nature of its law must be examined. Given God's revelation of himself most fully in Scripture, and the fact that he is the ultimate standard of morality in his creation, we must seek to apply the biblical pattern of morality and its enforcement in a "Christian" state. How, in doing this, do we discern what is to be legislated and what should not be? The Torah provides an extensive law that prohibits idolatry, false religion, murder, theft, manslaughter, adultery, sex outside of marriage, homosexuality, etc. If we enact that the full extent of the Torah's legal system, we are faced with a dilemma. At this point, there will be no one in our country to evangelize, the primary purpose of the Christian calling. All unbelief will be driven out of or punished within the Christian state. We then compromise our fundamental calling in pursuit of consistently Christian legislation. We are faced by the further dilemma that under the New Testament, we know

---

[11] Cf. the interplay between Saul, the king chosen by the people, and David, the king chosen by God in 1 Samuel. Cf. Rutherford, *God's Kingdom*.

that the Torah cannot be implemented wholesale (as discussed above). If we take up the stance of discriminating application, we have no biblical criteria for discerning what laws ought to be applied and what not to apply. For example, if we chose those that involve direct harm to others, such as theft and murder—and maybe adultery—we do so with no biblical authority. Furthermore, we are left with many activities that are legal and yet ultimately destructive to society, such as idolatry and homosexuality. Herein is the paradox: in enacting a truly Christian legal system we may not enact all the provisions of the Torah but have no biblical reason to discriminate between its provisions.

c. Paradox 3 – A Christian state cannot consistently permit the marketplace of ideas that gives a foothold for Christian evangelism.

The previous paradox leads us to another. For Christ's Church, manifest in local churches, to succeed in its purposes, it needs to be in and around unbelievers. Its purposes is to shine forth the glory of God in Christ so that they might see Christ and follow him; its purpose is to preach the Gospel so they might repent of their sins and entrust themselves to Christ. In his book *The Global Public Square*, Os Guinness argues for the political doctrine of "Soul Freedom," "the inviolable freedom of thought, conscience, religion and belief that lone does full justice to the dictates of our humanity."[12] I think he argues persuasively that this is a positive picture of society, a society in which the Christian mission can succeed. In a society that upholds "soul freedom," we will always have plenty of unbelievers in proximity and the freedom to demonstrate to them the glory of Christ. The farther we get from such a tolerant pluralism, the harder it will be to bring the gospel to our neighbours. So, we can identify a society shaped by this idea as an ideal context for Christian witness. Another context that would be difficult and yet yield much fruit would be a hostile environment, where Christian witness is illegal and so consistent Christian living will be thrown in sharp relief with unbelief.[13] However, the context where our witness would be most

---

[12] Os Guinness, *The Global Public Square: Religious Freedom and the Making of a World Safe for Diversity* (InterVarsity Press, 2013), 14.

[13] In my article "Benefits of Secularity," I argue that secularism in Western society may make Christian witness easier. It is true that the cost of witnessing will be higher: we are more likely to be rejected. However, it is easier to demonstrate with

ineffective would be one in which unbelief is not present or what unbelief is present is disguised. This is exactly the context that would emerge under a biblical Christendom. If we fight for a truly Christian state, and do so in a consistently biblical manner, we will end up driving away unbelievers and pushing those that remain into hiding. So here is the paradox: if we are consistently Christian in our political reformation, we will be inconsistently Christian in the purpose to which God has called us.

d. Paradox 4 – The Most Able Practitioners of Law will be the Ministers

One final paradox that I believe emerges is one we see in history. If the state is governed according to Scripture, then the best interpreters of Scripture will be its legislators or at least significant advisors for its legislation. If the ministers of the Gospel are those with exemplary moral character and the skills and practice necessary to interpret and apply God's Word, they are those most fit to draft and arbitrate the state's legislation. Under the Torah, the priests were charged with the highest level of legal arbitration and the king was expected to be thoroughly acquainted with the Law (Deut 16:18-17:20). Two problems emerge when ministers of the Gospel or potential ministers of the Gospel are drawn on for leadership in the state. In the latter case, there may be a shortage of leaders for the churches if they are culled for leadership in the state. In either case, the roles and activities of the civil magistrates and the Gospel ministers will become hard to distinguish, as both will be involved in the interpretation and application of Scripture. This will invite the confusion of the local church with its distinct mission and the state, a God governed yet Satanic entity. Furthermore, this will lead to the real temptation for corruption among the priesthood, as is witnessed throughout the history of the Church, where the bishops and ecclesiastical leaders have had great authority and influence in the state. Finally, there will be a very real temptation for ministers to be distracted from their calling. The reality of this temptation is attested in Scripture in response to a different concern; in Acts, we are told that the ministers of the Gospel were being distracted from their work of teaching by the physical needs of their congregations. To solve this problem, the apostles appointed deacons to serve these physical needs (Acts

---

our lives and words the difference the Gospel makes and how it genuinely points to a better, more joyful life than secularism. Rutherford, "Benefits of Secularity."

6:1-7). How much more will the danger of distraction be when the distraction is so similar to the actual calling of the minister? We can summarize the case against the Christian transformation of the state in this way: by focusing on doing good to others, we will end up endangering our proper calling, Christ's commission to his churches (cf. Gal 6:10).

So far, I have argued that Christians must submit to their governing authorities unless doing so would contradict their conscience. Furthermore, Christians must not seek to institute a Christian state on earth, lest they compromise God's purpose in this age. This leaves one loose end to address, at least as far as we are concerned in a book of this size. Is there any room for positive Christian engagement with the state, such as was seen in 18th and 19th century England with the abolition of slavery?

3) Christians make decisions with regard to the state according to conscience and its own (flawed) logic

Paul calls churches to focus on their primary calling, yet they are to "do good to everyone" as they have opportunity (Gal 6:10). If we cannot explicitly apply biblical reforms to our governments, do we have an opportunity do good to our neighbour through governmental reform? It should be clear that in the time of the New Testament and for the Old Testament exiles, this was a moot point. Given the pagan totalitarianism they faced, there was no room for biblical reforms. However, this is not our situation; within Western democracy, our votes and lobbying may effect actual change in our societies. Again, the question emerges, do Western democracy and its equivalents provide us with an opportunity "to do good to everyone?" I believe it does, but we must resort to the governing motif in this chapter, insurgency. An insurgent is someone functioning within an existing system for purposes alien to that system. We cannot function as true citizens, governed by the purposes of and allegiance to the state. Nor can we function as transformers, governed by the purposes, allegiances, and structures of an opposing state. Instead, we are left with the option of being governed by our Lord and his word within a system dictated by an antithetical purpose and its own logic.

Because all people in this world know God (Rom 1:18ff), the institutions they created will reflect reality and biblical revelation. However, because they distort this knowledge and attribute it to the created order, we can expect this truth to be held inconsistently and incoherently. That is, they will know truth but will fail to attribute it rightly to God; they will know truth but will not have a sufficient reason to hold it.[14] So the state will have its own inconsistent logic. Because this logic touches on the truth, we can employ that logic to fight for the truth as revealed to us in Scripture. Paul, for example, feels free to appeal to the Roman legal system and his rights within it to achieve a good purpose, a purpose in line with his divine calling (cf. Acts 25:6-12). God uses this to bring Paul to Rome. In the book of Daniel, we are not told that Daniel and his compatriots seek to reform Babylon according to the Bible, yet they witness to the one true God and represent him within this pagan society. They act according to the state's logic without contravening their conscience. In the Book of Esther, Esther transgresses the law of the Persians and the Medes to achieve God's purposes, to save the Jews, yet this act is one of following conscience, not of reforming the Persian legislation. The Jews to whom Jeremiah writes in Jeremiah 29 are called to live lives fitting to the context in which they live, Babylon, yet in continuity with their unique identity. We must be careful with Old Testament examples, for their purpose was to be a unique beacon of God's purposes within a concrete land, a purpose unattainable in Babylon. In contrast, our God-given purpose as the Church manifest in local churches is explicitly tied to our exile, to being in but not of the world. However, we do witness in the Old Testament examples of how God's people through the ages have related to secular states in submission to God's word. We simply have no examples in either testament of attempts to reform the state; what we have examples of and commands pertaining to is living in submission to authority, acting freely according to the internal logic of that state in as much as conscience is not contradicted.

It should be clear that in this section we are farthest from the clear teaching of Scripture than we have been thus far. However, I would like to suggest that this tension—living biblically according to a non-Biblical logic—allows us to make mild improvements to the state for the common good. For example, if a state rightly outlaws murder and recognizes the inherent dignity of human life, however they so define and defend these premises, we can rightly show that a consistent application of these principles would lead to

---

[14] Cf. Rutherford, *The Gift of Knowing*.

the restriction of abortion and infanticide. We should humbly acknowledge that this is probably not the best way to solve these horrid atrocities—abortion and infanticide have happened for millennia, even when illegal—but if we can bring even small victories in favour of the unborn in this manner, it may be wise to take such action. However, if doing so would compromise our primary purpose, such as identifying ourselves and Christianity with the government, alienating those we seek to reach, it may be wise to refrain from acting and trust that God is just to punish evildoers and act in favour of the widow and the orphan. Our calling is to do good to everyone, especially the weak and defenceless, but our primary purpose is to do good to the household of faith in order that the Gospel might go forth effectively and powerfully. We have confidence that God does care for the widow and orphan, the weak and the powerless, and he has repeatedly acted throughout history to achieve his purposes: the Church is *not* his primary instrument of civil reform. Similarly, the abolition of slavery was a good end, and if we had to fight that battle today and could do so according to the states internal logic, it would seem that this would be a wise and good action to take. Examples like this may be multiplied, but it should be clear that any action Christians take *vis-à-vis* the state must be done humbly, wisely, and with careful consideration of the church's primary purpose.

I hope it is clear how the position outlined here differs from the transformationalist and R2K approaches to the state. The above approach, appealing to the states "own logic" is different from the R2K approach in that it recognizes, first, that there is no coherent foundation for the secular state (we reject natural law) and, second, that the state is fundamentally opposed to God's saints even if we manage to coexist at times in history. I believe the preceding considerations would caution a Christian from pursuing roles in government and related entities, such as the military (and I believe other considerations would weigh in here as well). However, what happens when a politician, an emperor, or a business partner converts to Christianity?

C. What if the King Repents?

This is an important question to ask, for many of us turn to Christ late in life, after establishing a career. And in history, emperors have repented. Thankfully, we have some clear biblical guidance in these matters. First, Paul writes to believing spouses of unbelievers; he tells them that they should not seek to end that relationship but use it as an opportunity to make the Gospel known (1 Cor 7:12-16). They are not to demand their spouse conform to a biblical ethic (1 Cor 7:12-16, cf. 1 Cor 5:9-13), yet they are nevertheless to use this relationship as an opportunity for the Gospel (1 Cor 7:13-14). Second, Paul broadens the application of this principle—using an otherwise forbidden relationship for God's purposes (cf. 2 Cor 6:14-7:1)—in the following paragraph of the letter:

> Only let each person lead the life that the Lord has assigned to him, and to which God has called him. This is my rule in all the churches. Was anyone at the time of his call already circumcised? Let him not seek to remove the marks of circumcision. Was anyone at the time of his call uncircumcised? Let him not seek circumcision. For neither circumcision counts for anything nor uncircumcision, but keeping the commandments of God. Each one should remain in the condition in which he was called. Were you a bondservant when called? Do not be concerned about it. (But if you can gain your freedom, avail yourself of the opportunity.) For he who was called in the Lord as a bondservant is a freedman of the Lord. Likewise he who was free when called is a bondservant of Christ. You were bought with a price; do not become bondservants of men. So, brothers, in whatever condition each was called, there let him remain with God. (1 Cor 7:17-24)

Concerning slaves, Paul's prohibition is different from that concerning marriage: they may seek their freedom if the opportunity presents itself. However, the general teaching remains the same: new converts who find themselves in circumstances that would otherwise be unadvisable—some that are not biblically permissible—may and ought to use this position as an opportunity for the Gospel. Of course, there will be many situations where a new convert must leave their previous life entirely; such is the case when the previous situation is illegal or causes the person to engage in continual sin and so violates conscience.[15] So, I surmise, if the president, emperor, or prime minister—or any member of parliament—converts to Christianity, they

---

[15] I have found Calvin's comments in his Corinthians commentary sober and helpful in these regards. John Calvin, *Commentaries on the Epistles of Paul the Apostle to the Corinthians*, trans. John Pringle (Bellingham: Logos Bible Software, 2010).

ought to use their position for the Gospel in as much as is possible. Our previous considerations factor in at this point; they may not implement a wholesale Christian reformation, but they may use the logic of the state to achieve ends amicable to the God's commission to his churches. However, it would be inadvisable, given the whole biblical picture, to seek such a position in the first place. There may also be times where a leader in such a position will have to abdicate their role because remaining in the role would cause them to compromise their faith and violate conscience.

We have so far touched on an area of Christian living that is highly relevant to Christians living within a Western democracy. However, the implications of our discussion extend far beyond the borders of politics; I hope that the implications of our discussion of the church and the world thus far have provided fertile soil for thinking more clearly about biblical ethics and God's will in whatever particular situations you find yourselves in at this time. One issue that frequently emerges in a discussion such as this, an issue of particular concern to me and which affects Christian families in Western countries, is the question of education, particularly grade school education. Post-secondary education deserves its own treatment, but I believe the discussion below will indicate some areas for further thought in this regard.

D. Christians and Education

In his book *The Case for Classical Christian Education*, Douglas Wilson argues it is sinful for Christians to participate in the public education system: "Christian parents are morally obligated to keep their children out of government schools because the Scriptures expressly require a non-agnostic form of education."[16] I believe it is pastorally unwise to make such a sweeping statement, but I do agree with Wilson that the Bible has much to say about education and the need for Christian parents to give their children a God-centred education. However, there are many circumstances where parents will find it most wise to have their kids attend public schools, whether it is mandatory or because of the costs related to homeschooling or private education. In such cases, a Christian parent will have to work hard in the

---

[16] Wilson, *The Case for Classical Christian Education*. See my review in Appendix 2.

home to teach their child a Christian view of the world over against the non-Christian view they will receive in this context. What we can say is that parents have the mandate from God to teach their children the ways of the Lord.[17] When we marry this mandate with what we have learned about the state so far and with a general Christian view of life and of knowledge, we may begin to see how participation in the secular school system will often be unwise.

Though the Bible does not require us to give the broad education associated with contemporary Western education—including language studies, history, culture, math, and the physical sciences, among other things—it is legally a requirement in many countries to provide our children with comparable education, including in Australia and Canada. We are, by God's grace, currently free to pursue such education in the secular system, through private schools, or at home. Above we saw that the state is used by God but is fundamentally a participant in Satan's kingdom and opposed to God and his saints. From this alone, we should be wary of entrusting the early childhood formation of our children to the state. In practice, public education in the United States and Canada is rife with problems. In most cases, public schools do not provide a suitable atmosphere for the formation of a Christian worldview and Christian virtue. This often results in poor academic results also. Our goal for educating our child is not ultimately academic, though that is often helpful for their future. Instead, our goal ought to be to train our children in the ways of the Lord. In Deuteronomy 4:1-14 and chapter 6, Moses instructs the people to teach their children about the Lord, his mighty deeds, and his Law. Many of Israel's rituals were designed to raise teaching opportunities, opportunities to pass on knowledge of God's mighty acts in history and his demands in the present (e.g. the Passover). In Ephesians 6, Christian parents (here, fathers) are given the command to "bring [their children] up in the discipline and instruction of the Lord" (6:4). Given the legal requirement to educate our children (and the necessity of knowledge and skill to live in the modern world), we must ask, what method of education available to us best allows us to fulfil this command, best allows us to prepare our children to love and serve Jesus Christ, our Lord?

---

[17] Cf. Jay Edward Adams, "Christian Education: A Three-Walled Enterprise. (Editorial)," *Journal of Pastoral Practice 1979* (January 1, 1979).

In addition to its poor results in our age and its ideological struggles—not to mention its association with Satan's kingdom—there is another reason to question the public school system's compatibility with this task. Someone may suggest that they allow the public school system to equip their children with a knowledge of the world and their culture while they allow the church and their time as a family to equip them for life before God. But immediately a problem emerges; proportionally, is it right that most of a child's early life should be dedicated to skill and knowledge acquisition apart from Christ, especially if the Christian life is all-encompassing? Furthermore, is it the right message to give our kids if faith and devotion to Christ is an addition to eight hours a day, five days a week where his name and glory are absent? More importantly, a secular education system, a system that teaches everything without reference to God and his purpose through Christ will inevitably teach a worldview (provide a lens for interpreting and living within the world) that is contrary to the Christian worldview revealed in the Bible. Think about it for a moment. According to the Bible, all aspects of the created order were created to demonstrate his glory and all human history revolves around the kingdom of God manifesting through his Son. If we teach about the created order apart from this purpose, we are teaching a false view of it. When we learn mathematics, we are given a vision of an ordered universe and human mind; we are told *what is* apart from the fundamental reason *why it is that way*, namely, God and his faithfulness.[18] This may just lead us to believe that the world is fine without God. Something similar occurs with the sciences. In history, we are introduced to events and moments in history that are chosen not because of their significance for God's purposes but because of an arbitrary standard relative to our time and nation. We are also given an interpretation of these events that revolves around humanity and their purposes, not God and his purposes. If all life revolves around God and his purpose fulfilled through the Church, the children of Christ's people must be given a vision of the world consistent with this truth.

For these reasons, I do not believe a public education system is compatible with the Christian goal of education. My own conclusion is that home school, where possible, best fits the Christian goal of education, particularly because it maintains the authority structure of the family which

---

[18] Cf. Vern Sheridan Poythress, *Logic: A God-Centered Approach to the Foundation of Western Thought*, Electronic. (Wheaton: Crossway, 2013).

the Bible mandates for childhood and maintains parental responsibility in this essential task. However, an ideal is not always possible; Christians schools can be an adequate or even fantastic alternative. And with enough care and effort by parents, children can be adequately equipped despite a public education.

E. Conclusion

In this chapter we have looked at the Christian life and Christian interaction with secular society through the lens of soteriology. Christians are those who have been delivered from the domain of Satan, whose kingdom this world is. God's plan unfolding through history can be understood as cosmic warfare, in which the offspring of Satan oppose the offspring of woman, Eve. The former cultivate the created world for their own glory, but the latter seek to live before God in a faithful manner until he acts through his divine Son, the true offspring of the woman, to enact a perpetual kingdom of righteousness and justice within the creation. All our interactions with the world are thus viewed through the lens of this cosmic conflict: our role within this conflict is to fulfil God's purpose through faithful, whole-hearted commitment to the local church as it fulfils Christ's kingdom mandate (the great commission). We explored several significant areas of application for this theme.

Viewing the entire Christian life through this perspective, we could describe it as "insurgency": we have been sent far into enemy territory to lay the groundwork for the final victory when Christ returns. We live within enemy territory with the purpose of saving those who are at this time associated with the kingdom of darkness. Through the sharing of the Gospel, we hope to see them transferred to the glorious kingdom of Christ. Paul describes his ministry as that of reconciliation and the Christians role as "ambassadors," but we cannot imagine this as a peaceful exchange (5:11-6:13). Our weapons are not physical but spiritual, sufficient to remove obstacles to faith and commend Christ to those who hate him (Eph 6:10-20; 2 Cor 10:1-6). Because our task is preparatory and insurgent, we are not those entrusted with bringing final victory. This belongs to Christ alone; our hope lies in his imminent return when he will do away with all rebellion and create the heavens and earth anew as the place where he will dwell with his people. It is to this theme, eschatology, that we must now turn.

9

ESCHATOLOGY: EXILIC LIFE

Do not lay up for yourselves treasures on earth, where moth and rust destroy and where thieves break in and steal, but lay up for yourselves treasures in heaven, where neither moth nor rust destroys and where thieves do not break in and steal. For where your treasure is, there your heart will be also. – Matthew 6:19-21

Therefore let us go to him outside the camp and bear the reproach he endured. For here we have no lasting city, but we seek the city that is to come. – Hebrews 13:13-14

Eschatology is probably not a word that you would often associate with practical, biblical application. Instead, it is usually associated with speculation about orders of events, the identity of the antichrist, and the timing of Christ's return. Eschatology refers to the doctrine of end times; if we associate the "end times" with such things, we are failing to grasp the biblical use of the term. According to the New Testament, we are those upon whom the end of the age has come; we are living in the "end times" (1 Cor 10:11). The Old Testament has something scholars occasionally call a "collapsed eschatology"; that is, the Old Testament blends Jesus' first and last coming into a single event. Jesus coming is associated with the complete end of sin and the inauguration of an earthly rule. However, the New Testament reveals a new depth to God's plan for history; the end times are inaugurated with Christ's first coming but all the events that are identified with the "last times," "the end," and "latter days" happen between and after Christ's first and second coming. The New Testament, therefore, has what is sometimes called an "inaugurated eschatology," or the "already-not-yet" tension; the end times are here, yet they are not here in the full sense we read about in the Old Testament. This tension explains what we saw in the last chapter, where Satan is defeated and yet still active.

This is why we read that Jesus has finished the work and accomplished final victory (e.g. John 19:30; Col 2:15), yet Paul can say that his ministry is filling up "what is lacking in Christ's affliction" (Col 1:24). An analogy sometimes used is that of World War II; in a sense, the success of D-day guaranteed the victory at V-Day, though the latter was months to come. The period we live in is unique and has many implications for the Christian life. One way to capture our current state is with the picture of exile. Through Christ, we are guaranteed a future kingdom. Because our primary allegiance is due to him as our Lord, our King, we are citizens of his kingdom. We are citizens of his kingdom, yet that kingdom awaits us in the future; so, we are exiles or foreigners sojourning in foreign kingdoms until we arrive at the homeland we have been promised.

In one sense, like Abraham, we are "looking forward to the city that has foundations, whose designer and builder is God" (Heb 11:10). Yet, unlike Abraham, there is another sense in which we have come to the promised city:

> But you have come to Mount Zion and to the city of the living God, the heavenly Jerusalem, and to innumerable angels in festal gathering, and to the assembly of the firstborn who are enrolled in heaven, and to God, the judge of all, and to the spirits of the righteous made perfect, and to Jesus, the mediator of a new covenant, and to the sprinkled blood that speaks a better word than the blood of Abel. (Heb 12:22-24)

We have a foretaste of our heavenly inheritance through the church here in this world (cf. Chapter 7); however, we have not received the fulness of that inheritance: "Therefore let us go to him outside the camp and bear the reproach he endured. For here we have no lasting city, but we seek the city that is to come" (Heb 13:13-14). This brings us to the first eschatological perspective on the Christian life: our hope is future. Following this, we will consider the implications of Christ's final victory further and conclude with a reflection on his imminent return.

A. Our Kingdom, Our Hope, Is Future

Because our true home is the New Heavens and the New Earth, this world is not our home. This ought to challenge the way we think about our lives and possessions in this world; it is immensely freeing.

In the first case, we are challenged to not identify ourselves with any home here on earth. This means that however much we love the countries and cities in which we live, they must never possess our allegiance. The author of the 2nd century "Epistle to Diognetus" captures this well:

> [Christians] live in their own homelands but as aliens: they participate in everything as citizens but endure all things as strangers. Every foreign land is their homeland, and every homeland is foreign.[1]

We should always be less Canadian or American than we are Christian. There is a very real sense in which the world and its desires are passing away (1 John 2:17), so we cannot hold fastidiously to them. Many transformationalists emphasize the continuity between the present world and the world to come,[2] yet the clear teaching of Peter and John is that this present world will pass away with fire and a New Heaven and New Earth will be created in its place (2 Pet 3:8-13; Rev 21:1-8).[3] Because of the fleeting nature of this world,

> what sort of people ought you to be in lives of holiness and godliness, waiting for and hastening the coming of the day of God, because of which the heavens will be set on fire and dissolved, and

---

[1] My translation.

[2] N. T. Wright, *Surprised by Hope: Rethinking Heaven, the Resurrection, and the Mission of the Church*, 1st ed. (New York: HarperOne, 2008).

[3] Some argue that such an understanding misrepresents or fails to properly understand 2 Peter 3. There is a good text critical argument to be made that ουκ in 3:10 is not original, so that "the earth and its works will *not* be found" would be more accurately "the earth and the works done in it will be found." The meaning of this clause is not clear, explaining why the manuscript evidence is varied. However, given the context, this cannot mean less than that the old heavens and earth will be completely destroyed (3:11-13). Richard Bauckham is probably right to argue that this means "will be manifest" or "will be revealed." In the context of its utter destruction, the futility or fleeting nature of that the old world is what is manifest in its passing. Richard Bauckham, *Jude, 2 Peter* (Waco, Tex.: Word Books, 1983).

> the heavenly bodies will melt as they burn! But according to his promise we are waiting for new heavens and a new earth in which righteousness dwells. (2 Pet 3:11-13)

The fleeting nature of this world also challenges us to forsake earthly comfort and hope in earthly treasures for the sake of Christ. In addition to forsaking our very lives for the sake of Christ (cf. Luke 9), Jesus tells his people:

> Do not lay up for yourselves treasures on earth, where moth and rust destroy and where thieves break in and steal, but lay up for yourselves treasures in heaven, where neither moth nor rust destroys and where thieves do not break in and steal. For where your treasure is, there your heart will be also. (Matthew 6:19-21)

If our hearts are set on our true home, our home that is to come, our lives will look remarkably different.

In the second case, this gives us great comfort. If this world is fleeting, we do not have to be anxious over its turmoil and decaying state. The world will come to an end, and we know it will come to an end through Christ. We must not fear, therefore, a nuclear winter, the sudden death of our sun, nor a mass extinction of humanity through environmental degradation. I will leave it to those wiser than me to apply the principles elucidated in this book towards an account of the Scriptural mandate for our *actions* in regard to such things; however, what is clear is that these things must not cause us anxiety. Our hope and our future are not tied to this dying world, and no matter what we do, we cannot save it from its end. With all creation we recognize that this world will come to an end; instead of worrying or seeking to forestall that end, we long for the glory of the children of God:

> For I consider that the sufferings of this present time are not worth comparing with the glory that is to be revealed to us. For the creation waits with eager longing for the revealing of the sons of God. For the creation was subjected to futility, not willingly, but because of him who subjected it, in hope that the creation itself will be set free from its bondage to corruption and obtain the freedom of the glory of the children of God. For we know that the whole creation has been groaning together in the pains of childbirth until now. And not only the creation, but we ourselves, who have the firstfruits of the Spirit, groan inwardly as we wait eagerly for adoption as sons, the redemption of our bodies. For in

this hope we were saved. Now hope that is seen is not hope. For who hopes for what he sees? But if we hope for what we do not see, we wait for it with patience. (Rom 8:18-25)

Indeed, we long for this world to end and we ought to take action so that we might watch it burn, as Peter says, "waiting for and hastening the coming of the day of God, because of which the heavens will be set on fire and dissolved, and the heavenly bodies will melt as they burn!" (2 Pet 3:12). This does not mean triggering a world war, burning as many environmental pollutants as possible, or doing anything else to bring humanity's apocalyptic fears to reality; instead, this means living Godly, obedient lives, seeking to fulfil God's purpose. As we bring our purposes fully in line with his, as we seek holiness, the church's mission will be accomplished; in this manner, we hasten the coming victory of Christ.

B. We Have Confidence in Christ's Final Victory

And let us not be deceived, brothers and sisters, Christ will indeed have victory. We have the confidence to endure all things—including hardship and even death—because Christ has overcome the grave and will return to finish his work. Nothing in this life can separate us from his love (Rom 8:28-39); his work will assuredly be accomplished. We must endure this life, persevere through it, yet because Christ has victory, we have this great promise and challenge:

> Be faithful unto death, and I will give you the crown of life. He who has an ear, let him hear what the Spirit says to the churches. The one who conquers will not be hurt by the second death. (Rev 2:10-11)

Because Christ has the victory, we can proceed in our task with great confidence. As we preach the Gospel, hearts will be transformed by the Holy Spirit, and God's elect will respond to his voice. Christ's sheep will hear his voice, and "they will listen" (John 10:16):

> My sheep hear my voice, and I know them, and they follow me. I give them eternal life, and they will never perish, and no one will snatch them out of my hand. My Father, who has given them to

me, is greater than all, and no one is able to snatch them out of the Father's hand. (John 10:27-29)

Because Satan is bound and unable to deceive the nations (Rev 20:1-3), the Gospel will go forth with power to the gentiles. And when the fullness of us Gentiles have responded, God will call "all Israel" to himself (Rom 11:25-32). In this way, through the local church bringing the Gospel to the nations, God will draw all his sheep—Jew and Gentile—into one flock, with one shepherd (John 10:16). Jesus will attain final victory; we partake in his plan to bring about this victory. We do so with great confidence that in life or in death, his purpose will be accomplished. In the resurrection, we will receive the fulness of life, enjoying God forever in a new creation, free from sin. In light of Christ's assured victory, we live faithfully for him; we hear his promise, "Surely I am coming soon," and we cry out with the rest of the saints, "Amen. Come, Lord Jesus!" (Rev 22:20).

C. We Live in Expectation of Christ's Imminent Return

This brings us to the last eschatological perspective with which we need to look at Christian life within the world. We must live in expectation of and with urgency in light of Christ's return. The pervasive picture presented in the New Testament is that Christ is at the door. The last act of history is his return, and he could come at any time.[4] In addition to his words at the end of Revelation and throughout the book (e.g. Rev 3:11), we see the same thing in James 5:8-9, Hebrews 10:25, Philippians 4:5, and 1 Peter 4:7. Jesus is very clear about the matter;

> From the fig tree learn its lesson: as soon as its branch becomes tender and puts out its leaves, you know that summer is near. So also, when you see all these things, you know that he is near, at the very gates. Truly, I say to you, this generation will not pass away until all these things take place. Heaven and earth will pass away,

---

[4] For a further defense of this point, see my paper "Coming on the Clouds." https://teleioteti.ca/papers/.

but my words will not pass away. (Matt 24:32-35)

"All these things" refers to the destruction of the temple (AD 70); with this out of the way, Christ could return at any moment.[5] We have seen the leaves, now we know "he is near, at the very gates." Jesus expectations are very clear in this regard, "Therefore you also must be ready, for the Son of Man is coming at an hour you do not expect" (Matt 24:44). That Christ could come back at any moment means that we must always be ready, working out our faith with fear and trembling. Paul appeals to the immanence of Christ to call congregations to make the most use of their time for the sake of the Gospel (Rom 13:11-14; 1 Cor 7:29; cf. Eph 5:15-16). Christians are those who have found rest from their sin and the labours of a futile world (Matt 11:28-30, Heb 4:1-13), yet walking with Christ is its own labour and we undertake it with a sense of urgency, knowing that the time is short. When Christ returns, God's patience will have been spent; no opportunity for repentance will be found. Thus, we act towards this fallen world with a sense of its impending judgment. We take the truth seriously that all who are apart from Christ at his return will stand before their judge and be found wanting. We must labour with all our might and effort to build up the local church in order that God's purpose in this world might be fulfilled. Eschatology is both our hope and our challenge to do this.

---

[5] Ibid.

CONCLUSION

All authority in heaven and on earth has been given to me. Go therefore and make disciples of all nations, baptizing them in the name of the Father and of the Son and of the Holy Spirit, teaching them to observe all that I have commanded you. And behold, I am with you always, to the end of the age. – Matthew 28:18-20

Here we are, having travelled far, but I hope the journey has been rewarding. We have undertaken the task of investigating Christian purpose and identity in this world. In interaction with the question, "Should we save the West?" we have sought biblical questions concerning the Christian posture towards the West specifically and the whole world by extension. I hoped that by taking this approach, we might move beyond the paradigmatic approaches of Niebuhr's *Christ and Culture*. I hoped that we would consider the tapestry of practical biblical instruction and its portrayal of history to a greater depth.

In Part 1, we considered history briefly; I suggested that Western culture was not worth saving after all. In Part 2, we considered several different positive approaches to Western culture. In Chapter 4, we considered the strategy of ressourcement in three manifestations. In each case, we argued that these approaches overestimated our Western heritage and failed to take the sufficiency of Scripture seriously. In Chapter 5, we examined transformationalism, the belief that Christians ought to see Christ's kingdom manifest here and now in a tangible Christendom. Again, we found the Scriptural foundation for this approach wanting. In Chapter 6, we turned to the Reformed Two Kingdoms approach, the last position we would consider. Here, we considered the value of natural law and the distinction between the common and redemptive kingdom. Though none of these positions was completely wrong, they each brought some Scriptural applications into a paradigm that failed to do justice to the whole picture. This brought us to Part 3, a constructive proposal. Here, we did not and have not presented a paradigm for interpreting the Christian approach to secular society. Instead, we examined three biblical themes—which I believe to be the most important themes in this regard. Looking at ecclesiology, we saw how God's purposes centre on the local church and how the local church in its gatherings and daily activities is the locus of his saving work in this world. Looking at soteriology, we saw how God's kingdom is breaking into hostile territory, a kingdom ruled by Satan; our task within the local church was thus contextualized as part of cosmic warfare. Here we considered how this antithesis of hostile kingdoms provides an important perspective on several key issues in Christian ethics. Finally, in chapter 9, we considered eschatology, the doctrine of the last days. We saw that we are citizens of an eschatological kingdom ruled by Christ, citizens in exile among a world passing away. We looked at the way our hope for a future kingdom, our confidence in Christ's victory, and the urgency of his imminent return shapes and strengthens our conviction as we pursue God's mission through the local church.

All of us should be challenged by what we have seen. None of us loves the local church enough and lives with the holiness—with the radical commitment to God's purposes—that Christ calls us to. Christ has called us to take up our cross and follow him; I hope what we have seen indicates some of the radical ways we need to die to our desires and ambitions if we hope to follow Christ. Thanks be to God that we will not be judged according to the works we have done in this life, for all of us would be found wanting. Our only hope in light of our failings and our hope to persevere in growing faithfulness day by day is the promise that God made him who knew no sin to be sin on our behalf (2 Cor 5:21). We hope that when we stand before our judge on the final day, we will not be measured by the books containing all the works done on this earth but by the book of the life of the lamb who was slain (Rev 20:11-15).

We ought to be challenged, yet I hope we have seen that we can also have great confidence in God's provision for life in this world. The Word of

God has a lot to say for our situation and the decisions we make in this world. From each theme we considered, we saw how Scripture is sufficient for the Christian life. It does not tell us how to be a mechanic, but it does tell us if and how we ought to use our skills as a mechanic to further Christ's purpose on earth. It portrays a universe upheld by God so that the work of a mechanic can be performed and indicates that such work has value in as much as it supports the work of the church and does not burden it; it may also count as a good done to everyone. Scripture is sufficient because it gives us everything of substance for our lives and what is necessary for every good work. Being a mechanic or a mom may be a good work, or it may not be. Scripture gives us what is necessary for it to be a *good* work. It contextualizes every decision and every action within an unfolding vision of history, where God's work reaches its climax in Christ and finds its end at his return. It shows us that the local church ought to be the focus of our endeavours. Finally, it shows us that we do not have to solve the crises of our age. Instead, we must look for and hope in the coming of our Lord Jesus Christ to bring an end to injustice and futility.

In conclusion, let's consider once again our purpose. God has entrusted his church with the task of spreading his Gospel through faithful witness, proclamation of the Gospel, and the building up of Christians to obey Christ:

> All authority in heaven and on earth has been given to me. Go therefore and make disciples of all nations, baptizing them in the name of the Father and of the Son and of the Holy Spirit, teaching them to observe all that I have commanded you. And behold, I am with you always, to the end of the age. (Matt 28:18-20)

PART 4

Appendices

APPENDIX 1: REVIEW OF EMPIRES OF DIRT[1]

For the last several years, I have spent a lot of time thinking through the question, how do we, as Christians, live within and respond to culture? As I have worked out these issues, I have had Douglas Wilson's *Empires of Dirt* recommended to me a couple of times. The freedom of a PhD program, Coronavirus lockdown, and the occasion of a new book project on the subject has given me the opportunity to give it a read and review. In sum, I was not persuaded that Wilson's "Mere Christendom" is a biblical ideal. For this review, I will offer a brief summary of the book and evaluation. The evaluation section will be a touch longer than usual, because of my current interest in the topic at hand, but a full address of the issues involved in Wilson's proposal will have to await the project mentioned above.

Summary: Towards a Mere Christendom

Essentially, Wilson wants to offer a postmillennial political alternative to the extremes of Secularism and Radical Islam. Secularism is the false claim to religious neutrality in the public square; in reality, it is an alternate religion that does not proclaim the Lordship of Christ. Radical Islam is the totalitarian claims of Allah and his prophet over all life, including the state. Wilson's alternative is a "mere Christendom," "a network of nations bound together by a formal, public, civic acknowledgement of the lordship of Jesus Christ

---

[1] Wilson, *Empires of Dirt*.

and the fundamental truth of the Apostle's Creed" (pg. 7, loc. 101).[2] his focus is America, his home, and the prospects for achieving this goal in this nation. He does not envision a drastic revolution but a slow, patient change brought about by churches and Christians living faithfully and interacting in the political sphere in submission to Christ (195-196, loc. 2473-2488). There is a general progression in his argument, but it is not purely linear. It involves general meditations on these themes—Secularism, Radical Islam, and Mere Christendom.

Chapter 1 & Chapter 3 take up Secularism and Radical Islam, with a particular focus on Wilson's American context. Secularism in America is the false religion of American Exceptionalism, or Americanism. Chapters 2, 4, and 5 address alternative Christian proposals to these two extremes. Chapter 2 considers "Christ and Culture," concluding that anything less than Christ's total Lordship over the world proclaimed and lived out is unchristian. Chapter 4 considers the Anabaptist approach to culture, an approach that Wilson identifies in many of his Reformed peers. Wilson picks Gregory Boyd as his conversation partner for this chapter. Chapter 5 is the most extensive interaction with an opposing view, arguing against the Reformed Two Kingdoms position. Interacting particularly with Jason Stellman's *Dual Citizen* and James Hunter's *To Change the world: The Irony, Tragedy, and Possibility of Christianity in the Late Modern world*, Wilson argues that the Two Kingdoms view is inconsistent with historical Reformed theology and is essentially unliveable.

In the remaining chapters, Wilson argues for and explains his "Mere Christendom" proposal. His positive argument is grounded in the present reign of Christ and his Lordship over all things and the postmillennial view that history is inevitably progressing towards the full realization of God's kingdom on Earth. He places emphasis on the clause "to the nations" in the great commission, namely, the call to teach and baptize all nations, taken to be "the people, the tribe, the whole unit" (pg. 94, Loc. 1204). This includes calling for and seeing kings repent and seeking to declare and establish Christ's authority in these nations. He correlates this passage with the many Old Testament references to Christ's eternal reign over all nations. This is

---

[2] All references are to the page numbers and locations of the kindle edition.

what Wilson attempts, but I am not persuaded by his proposal.

Evaluation of a Mere Christendom Proposal

My issues with Wilson's *Empires of Dirt* are extensive, but I will restrict myself to commenting on three areas: 1) the nature of Wilson's rhetoric and argument; 2) his exegesis (and lack thereof) of biblical texts; 3) and the problems of applying Wilson's proposal.

The Argument and Rhetoric of Empires

As I mentioned already, I found Wilsons' argument to be unclear. The book would be a lot stronger if there was a careful map explaining the structure and progression of the book's argument. In addition to a generally unclear progression, Wilson's writing style is very aggressive. Elsewhere he has defended the use of satire, but the "serrated edge" of his rhetoric is uncharitable and does not commend itself to those who are unsympathetic to Wilson's proposal. Perhaps as a result of his style, Wilson's treatment of alternate approaches is neither charitable nor rigorous; often the object of his criticism is a straw man. For example, it is untenable to suggest that only a postmillennial transformationalist approach can justify its belief in the Lordship of Christ. I agree with Wilson that the anabaptist approach proposed by Boyd and the Reformed Two Kingdoms views are not consistently biblical, yet I can appreciate what they are attempting. At least with regard to the R2K view (this acronym stands for "Radical Two Kingdoms" in Wilson's parlance), Meredith Kline, Michael Horton, David VanDrunen, et al. legitimately see their view as a holding a robust view of Christ's Lordship and have some biblical reason for thinking so. In each case, it appears to me that Wilson fails to sympathize with or "enter" the perspective of these thinkers and understand *why* they say what they are saying. I believe he is right in identifying many weaknesses in the R2K position, but his critique does not come across as careful, considered, or generous. In these ways, Wilson appears to be speaking to the choir. His argument will resonate with those already sympathetic to his position but will not persuade many who are aligned otherwise. Beyond just the manner of argument, the use of Scripture in *Empires* contributes to this general unpersuasiveness.

The Exegesis of Empires

For a book seeking to offer a biblical proposal over against the unbiblical, even "heretical," positions of American Secularism and Radical Islam, *Empires of Dirt* is lacking in thorough biblical argument. The first interaction with Scripture begins on Page 78 (Loc. 974, almost a third of the way into the book). Here, Wilson interacts with Boyd's claim that "Jesus three times refers to Satan as the 'ruler of this world' (John 12:31; 14:30; 16:11)." Boyd understands "ruler" to be a distinctly political word, so Satan is the *political ruler* of the entire world. Wilson counters that Boyd is picking up on the word and not actually dealing with "what the verses he cites are actually *saying*" (78, Loc. 974). Is Boyd totally wrong, though? Wilson argues that in context, Satan is "cast out," "judged," and has "no claim on" Christ. Does this mitigate Boyd's point? The difficulty here is that later in the New Testament, Satan is still called the "ruler" and even "god" of this world (2 Cor 4:4; Eph 2:2, 6:4). This is the case, even after Satan has been bound (Mark 3:27, Rev 20:1-3) and cast out of heaven (Luke 10:18).

This is not simply a case of what these verses "are actually saying"; instead, Boyd and Wilson have alternate interpretations of Jesus' defeat of Satan. Revelation 20 and Mark 3 are clear about what they mean: Satan is bound with reference to deceiving "the nations"; Satan being bound, Christ can plunder his kingdom. Wilson's reference to the D-day landing in Normandy is actually a fitting analogy for what is going on here: on the Cross, Christ secured victory over Satan and made provision for the Gospel to go forth to all peoples—gentiles and Jews alike (see the context of John 12:31). Jesus' final victory is guaranteed but not yet realized in this world. The book of Revelation echoes Ephesians 6:4 in describing the entire span of history from now until Christ's return as one of warfare between Satan—thrown out of heaven but still at the helm of Babylon—and the people of God, persecuted yet enduring for the Sake of Christ. This warfare comes to an end when Christ comes on the clouds, strikes down Babylon, and throws Satan and his followers into the lake of fire (Revelation 19-21). In essence, the problem is not exegesis—though in the case of these verses, I am sympathetic to Boyd—but the overarching paradigm of what Christ's present reign means and how his heavenly rule will be realized on earth. The few texts to which Wilson turns to make the positive argument for his postmillennial interpretation are unpersuasive.

First, he makes much of the use of "the nations" in the great commission (94-95, Loc. 1199-1215). However, rarely in the New Testament—or the entire Bible—does "nation" refer to anything like a modern social-political nation. In a sense, a "nation" in the Bible describes some sort of unity among diverse peoples: it could be an ethnic unity, a kingdom, a religious group, etc. Often in the New Testament, especially in the plural ("the nations"), it means the non-Jewish world ("gentiles"). So, when Jesus says that Christians are to go out and make disciples of the nations, he does not mean socio-political entities but all people in all their diverse social standings, ethnicities, locations, and current religious affiliations (cf. Matt 6:32, 25:32; Mark 13:10; Luke 12:30; Luke 24:47; etc.). No implications can be drawn from this commission for Wilson's "Mere Christendom" proposal; the Great Commission is neither an argument against it (unless an argument of conspicuous absence) nor an argument for it.

Second, he argues that the portrait of New Jerusalem in Revelation 21 represents "the Christian Church, being gradually manifested through the course of history," not "a figure of Heaven, the final eternal state" (80-81, Loc 997-1014). I wholeheartedly agree that Revelation's "New Jerusalem" is the Church (not the Christian Church, however: it is God's people throughout history). However, it is both the Church AND the final state. That is, in Revelation, the New Jerusalem is not the Church "gradually manifested"; it is the Church perfected. Revelation is notoriously unchronological; however, the vision of New Jerusalem descending from Heaven is clearly indicated as the final state. In the preceding chapters, John's cyclical description of the history of the Church Age comes to a climactic end with the definitive description of Christ's victory, in Revelation 19-20. After Christ destroys the forces opposing his rule and people, we are told of the resurrection and final judgment (Revelation 20). After Satan is finally defeated (Rev 20:7-10, a recapitulation of Revelation 19), every opponent of God is thrown into the lake of fire, the second death. This is the final state for unbelievers. In addition to this vision (καὶ, and), John sees a vision of "a new heaven and a new earth" (21:1). The old creation has passed away, and all rebellion has ceased (21:1); in this context, he sees "the holy city, the new Jerusalem, coming down out of heaven from God."

All opposition to God is outside of this city, in the lake of fire (e.g. 21:8): it is not being gradually manifested but is climactically revealed at the end of the age. This does indeed have political implications (81, Loc. 1014), but these are not the implications Wilson sees. It is only after Christians have endured persecution that they are raised to new life and enjoy Christ's glorious and eternal kingdom (21:7); it is at this time that all the nations are struck down and shattered like clay pots (Rev 19:15; 2:26-27). Far from a gradual manifestation of God's kingdom, it appears to me that Christ's Kingdom on earth will be inaugurated in the climactic revelation of Christ from Heaven for the sake of his people spread throughout and persecuted in the world.

In these ways, I found the general lack of biblical interaction detrimental to Wilson's project and what interaction he offered was not sufficient to convince the unconvinced. The last issue I found in Wilson's project is the general untenability of transformationalist proposals, an untenability that Wilson does not address.

Applying the Mere Christendom Proposal

Empires of Dirt is thorough in explaining the big picture of its proposal: Christ's reign will be progressively realized in this world, and we should explicitly seek this through faithful Christian living towards a "Mere Christendom." However, other than limited comments on the limitations of state government, Wilson does not work out what exactly an earthly kingdom constructed within biblical parameters would look like. However, this is where I think the proposals for Christendom in any form have the most difficulties; they work well as an implication of eschatology but are incompatible with a careful exegesis of Scripture.

First, to apply Scripture to a Mere Christendom, we need to have a biblical theology of the state and understanding of its relation to the Old and New Testaments (unless we want to follow the Two Kingdoms crew in leaving it to natural revelation). Wilson suggests that the Bible teaches three distinct spheres of government that cannot overlap: Family, Church, and state (192-193, loc 2445-2457). However, in my reading of the New Testament, the Church overlaps and takes priority over the family in several significant ways (e.g. Matt 19:29-30). Furthermore, the relationship between these three is not clear: John Frame has argued that the Church and state are both evolutions of the Family, meaning that these are not so distinct.[3]

Second, it is clear in Wilson's proposal that he does not want to directly apply the Torah to a nation. However, if theocracy is the goal, it is hard to fathom how it could not be built on God's governmental revelation *par excellence*. If God's earthly kingdom once permitted divorce, given the nature of the fallen world, why would a new earthly kingdom make it illegal (221, Loc 2787)? If God's first kingdom penalized homosexuality, adultery, and fornication with death (Lev 18:7-23; 20:10-21), how could the new earthly kingdom not do so? The same issue applies to a child cursing their parents (Lev 20:6-9). If God's first kingdom penalized unbelief with death, how could his second kingdom not do so (Lev 24:10-16; Deut 7:17-26; Deut 13:1-18; 16:21-17:7)? Also, why would the physical symbols of God's distinctly Holy people (food laws, laws of dress) not apply to a new physically distinct people?

The biggest issue of application I see, however, pertains to the ruler. If Christ is the true King, finally enthroned at the right hand of the Father in fulfilment of God's promises to David and Abraham, how can any earthly ruler (king, president, prime minister, etc.) take the mantle of God's earthly kingdom? Furthermore, if we could establish some justification for this position, how would we know whom God has appointed to this role? In the Old Testament, theocracy required explicitly ordained leadership; election by the people was not looked upon favourably (Deut 17:14-20; cf. 1 Samuel 8-15, particularly 8:1-22).

We saw earlier several difficulties that emerge in the context of thinking through the application of the Bible to a "Christian kingdom." It is because of these paradoxes—along with the general tenor of the New Testament and the book of Revelation—that I find a proposal for a new Christendom untenable. It is a truly massive issue to consider how we as Christians can live faithfully in this world; Wilson has presented some helpful criticisms of Anabaptist and Reformed 2 Kingdoms approaches to the question, but his

---

[3] Frame, *The Doctrine of the Christian Life*, 595–602.

positive proposal is unclear where clarity is needed most, and his argument for it is unpersuasive.

APPENDIX 2: REVIEW OF THE CASE FOR CLASSICAL CHRISTIAN EDUCATION[1]

I am very interested in the subject of education, specifically, with the training of pastors and leaders for the Church. I have read extensively and thought deeply on this subject for a while now. Ever since I found out we were going to have a child two years ago, that interest in education has broadened to the topic of education throughout life, teaching children and adults. I have had serious concerns about the nature and very concept of state-run and secular education, so I have spent much time studying alternative Christian approaches to Childhood education. I first encountered Classical Christian education on thegospelcoalition.org, and then became concerned through the brief discussion of the movement in the book *Media, Journalism, and Communication*.[2] Since then, I have been looking for the opportunity to read more on the movement. Wilson's work seems to be highly influential, and the whole approach is closely tied to a book I am currently writing on Christian living in Western culture, so now seemed as good a time as any to give it a shot. In this review, I will offer a summary of the contents of *The Case for Classical Education* and then provide an evaluation of its content.

---

[1] Wilson, *The Case for Classical Christian Education*.

[2] Schuchardt, *Media*.

Summary

Douglas Wilson has written several books about education and the "Classical Christian" approach. *The Case for Classical Christian Education* brings together the themes of these books into a single volume offering a broad overview of Classical Christian Schools and offering a programme for their implementation. Through a critique of the current state of education and a presentation of the Classical Christian Approach, Wilson hopes to offer "a call for continued reformation of education in our country."[3] Overall, I think that Wilson fails to demonstrate why his model is biblical and an acceptable Christian alternative to the contemporary crisis of public education. There is some value in his critique of contemporary public education and the occasional practical insight for teaching from a Christian perspective. Still, overall, the book is ineffective for its stated goal. Furthermore, the argument and outline are not clear and, as I have observed in a previous review of Wilson's work, the rhetoric Wilson uses is not persuasive or becoming of Christian charity and clarity.[4]

The Logos edition I read was divided into 30 chapters and seven parts. The first eight chapters, making up the first part, present a broad criticism of government schools and the ideology that drives them. The next three parts (chapters 9-19) outline the Classical Christian School approach, in contrast with the government system. The final three parts (chapters 20-30) seem to offer a call and programme for implementing the Classical Christian approach in a local setting.

Evaluation

Though there are helpful insights throughout, and the critique of the public education system is often right on the mark, I did not find *The Case* to a balanced, persuasive, or carefully argued book. For example, the first comments Wilson makes about the public-school system are a broad condemnation of its use of "drugs." This section lacks any citations or

---

[3] The Logos Edition I read does not have page numbers

[4] See Appendix 1.

research backing it, so it comes across as anecdotal and not considered. The topic itself is a large one; there is undoubtedly a problem, but it is a lot more complicated than just blaming drugs. As a student, I was prescribed a significant behaviour-altering medication (Dexedrine) and had a negative experience with it; in hindsight, this was surely a case of over-prescription. However, can we be sure that this is the case every time? Like many issues in our contemporary culture, this topic takes far more sensitivity and nuance than Wilson offers. This lack of sensitivity and nuance is characteristic of Wilson's rhetoric throughout the book. For example, I largely agree that public schools (in my own country, Canada, and in the USA) are a mess and I think it is unwise to trust them for our children's education. However, it is equally unwise—and highly unpastoral—to say that putting your child in public school is a sin. As leaders, we can counsel our congregations in wise action. However, if in good conscience they put their children in the public school system, I see no clear biblical reason to identify this as sin. His comments about God's ordering the world hierarchically, such that each person has a fixed station, and his desire to see a high tuition charged to parents suggests that his "Christian" approach to education is only for a small portion of Christians. It seems to be pastorally irresponsible to call public education a sin, reject homeschooling as problematic, and suggest that the best alternative ought to be put out of reach for the average Christian family. One gets the impression that the education intended to equip Christian, covenant children for life before God should be reserved for the upper classes of such children. I think the exegetical warrant for such a position is lacking and the rhetoric employed highly unhelpful. Examples such as these could be multiplied.

Lack of Exegetical Warrant

This brings us to the biggest issue I found with the book, the lack of exegetical warrant for Wilson's proposal. One the hand, there is not a lot of actual biblical argumentation for the "Classical *Christian*" approach to education. Wilson's argument for it is largely based on historical precedence. When he does turn to the Bible, his exegesis is not strong. For example, "nations" (εθνη) in the great commission does not refer to "nation" in the modern sense of the word, so it cannot be used to justify the conversion of culture in Christendom.⁵ The commission refers to the evangelization and discipleship of all sorts of people, not nation-states (whatever it might mean to baptize and teach a nation-state). Also, it is exegetically irresponsible to import the whole concept of ancient Greek παιδεια (*paideia*) into the use of this word in Ephesians 6:4. This passage cannot on any reasonable exegesis of its context be used a call for formulating and providing a particularly Christian "παιδεια" (on analogy with the Greek concept). Instead, the ESV is right to translate the word "discipline." Also, even if one concludes that the promise cited by Paul here (Eph 6:1-3) is still in effect—which is not the only possible reading of this passage—the life promised is the New Covenant promise of Eternal Life, not the possession of the earth. It is also exegetically irresponsible to suggest that the Proverbs 22:6 can be used in a *modus tollens* syllogism, such that if a child does depart from the way, it is the parents' fault. This neglects the nature of a proverb (it is not a promise but a generalization of life in covenant before God) and neglects personal responsibility, a clear biblical teaching. Lastly, the concepts of "knowledge," "understanding," and "wisdom" in the Proverbs cannot be neatly correlated with the Trivium's "grammar, dialectic, and rhetoric." This brings us to the final point of evaluation I want to offer, on the overall proposal and its theological foundation.

General Issues with the Proposal

Apart from clear exegetical support, the primary theological justification for Wilson's proposal is postmillennial eschatology. If God's will is for an earthly Christendom and this is guaranteed through the progressive spread of the Gospel and Christian civilization on earth, then it makes sense that training Christians to live for God involves training them to live in and transform culture. Furthermore, on such a theology, the appeal Wilson makes to providence—such that the relationship between the West and Christianity is normative—is justified. However, if the reader rejects postmillennial eschatology, as this reader does, then there is no good reason to accept Wilsons' proposal. If you do accept a postmillennial vision of reality, I would still ask if we Reformed Christians should be content with a proposal that is consistent with our theology but has no clear exegetical foundation? If the

---

⁵ See Appendix 1

Bible is truly sufficient for every good work (2 Tim 3:16-17), should we not expect the Bible to clearer on these matters? I think the Bible has a lot to say about education and the parent's responsibility for it; I believe it would point in the direction of homeschooling for at least part of a child's education.[6]

As for the overall proposal, to fully address all the possible issues I see with this approach would take a book arguing for an alternative proposal (maybe I will get to it one day, or someone will beat me to it). However, I will raise three concerns. First, Wilson seems to reject all Enlightenment and post-enlightenment culture as bad, calling for a return to the pre-enlightenment culture of Augustine and the early Church. However, as much as we can respect Augustine and the early Church, it must be recognized that they were heavily influenced by Greek thought, thought that is as pagan as modern thought. There is no consistent reason to accept their Christianised Hellenism and reject Christianised modernism or postmodernism. Instead, what is needed is careful, biblical interaction with all of these movements. We live in a Postmodern world, so we as Christians need to address Postmodern issues. Many Postmodern writers help us do this. Modern thought and Postmodern thought also have given us great insight into the way God has created us and our minds; thus we can learn a lot about education from the last 300 years of philosophy and science—even psychology.[7] We must tread with care and submit all things before the Bible. We need to be thoroughly biblical, but we need to be biblically prepared to answer the questions and concerns of our age, not Augustine's, lest our children be unprepared for the world in which they actually live.

Second, Wilson argument for Latin is unpersuasive and misses a huge opportunity. Latin is a beautiful language, but if we are teaching our children responsible language use, it will not help them master English.[8] Many great

---

[6] Wilson addresses homeschooling briefly but does not address the exegetical warrant for it, namely, that the Bible identifies a child's education as the *parents'* responsibility.

[7] If I am right in identifying Van Tillian presuppositionalism at the root of Wilson's approach, it should be observed that Van Til is more in line with Postmodern thought than Modern or Premodern thought.

[8] E.g. *"nescius"* will not teach you the meaning of "nice"; *"ambulo"* will not help you understand *"ambulance"*; simply, etymology is not a good way to learn most

books in Church history are in Latin, yet only a handful of scholars will practically use Latin in this way (confession: I am a PhD student in theology with some training in Latin; I do not use it much and do not see myself using it much more than I do). Latin is also not better suited for logical thinking than English: the case system allows some precision in communication, yet English word order suffices for this. Furthermore, the case system does not give any ontological insights into the nature of reality or logic (such that knowing the ablative case would allow you to know the true meaning of prepositions). Indeed, English is more precise in some ways because of the use of the definite and indefinite article (Latin does not have an article). All of Wilson's goals could be met if his school taught *Koine* Greek and biblical Hebrew. In this way, the student would be exposed to different ways of expressing concepts and stories and thinking about logic, and they would be equipped to read the Bible in all the richness of its original languages. From this point, if the student wanted to specialize in Latin, Ancient Greek, Arabic, Syriac, Aramaic, or Modern Hebrew, they would have a broad foundation for doing so.

Lastly, Wilson's provides no more than anecdotal evidence for the use of the Trivium in education: is this adequate justification for using it? It seems to me that it could be as much a case of fitting the foot to the shoe as it is fitting the shoe to the foot; that is, the system may work because it is merely adequate and not because it is the ideal or best way to teach students. Linguistics offers a similar threefold analysis of human communication that may offer different insights, and some information theorists offer a five-fold analysis: either approach may work better than the Trivium's threefold analysis. However, it seems to me that all these levels interlock even in a child's understanding; could we be missing an opportunity by postponing analysis and presentation until Junior or High school ages? All this to say, there is no good philosophical, empirical, or biblical reason to believe that the Trivium is better than any educational insights we might glean from the Bible or contemporary thought. It is not hard to beat contemporary education, but merely doing better than what we have been doing should not be our goal. Doing the best to equip our children for life before God in this world should be the contemporary Christian educator's goal.

---

languages, especially when they have a complicated history, as English does.

Towards this end, a lot more thinking can be and should be put into the nature, goals, methods, and content of education aimed towards training our children for kingdom living. I am thankful that people are thinking about these matters but let's not be content with retrieving the past; looking to Scripture, let's do our best to meet the needs of our children in the present and the future with all the tools God has given us—including the insights of Modernism and Postmodernism.

APPENDIX 3: REVIEW OF THE CITY OF GOD AND THE GOAL OF CREATION[1]

The concept of "city" has long been of interest to theologians and biblical scholars, from Augustine's apology for the destruction of Rome and account of the war between the City of Man and the City of God (*The City of God*) to contemporary interest in cities among Christian sociologists (e.g. Jacques Ellul). For this reason, I was pleased to receive a copy of T. Desmond Alexander's *The City of God and the Goal of Creation*, the newest instalment of Crossways series *Short Studies in biblical Theology*.[2] The book was a rewarding read in many ways, yet it left this reviewer with the impression that something significant was missing.

Summary

As with all the contributions to this series, *The City of God* is written to make the recent scholarly work on biblical theology available to a wider lay-Christian audience. Biblical theology is concerned with the study of the Bible as a cohesive whole, often with a particular interest in the themes that run throughout it and that display its unity. Alexander thus tracks the concept of

---

[1] Alexander, *The City of God and the Goal of Creation*.

[2] I received a copy of *The City of God and the Goal of Creation* as part of Crossway's Blog Review Program.

"city" from Genesis to Revelation. He argues that the appearance of cities is by no means incidental, for at the heart of God's plan for creation is "an extraordinary city," which "God has graciously and patiently been working to create..., where he will dwell in harmony with humanity" (15-16).[3] In the book's eight concise chapters, Alexander traces the theme of the City of God and its antithesis, Babel or Babylon, by interacting book-by-book with significant passages that pertain to the theme. This is where the strength of the book is most evident; the engaged reader will walk away from *The City of God* with a better understanding both of the greater unity of Scripture through one of its key themes and of many individual books and passages. Alexander engages with Scripture proficiently, and his treatment of Sinai and the tabernacle should prove particularly illuminating to readers unfamiliar with the Old Testament and its religious system ("cultus"). There is, however, something missing from Alexander's treatment.

Evaluation

As with many works on biblical theology, orientated as they are to the description of the bible rather than its application, the reader is often left wondering what exactly the significance of an exposition or insight is. This is the biggest deficiency of the book. It could largely have been remedied by providing early on—or anywhere—a definition or explanation of what a city is and why it matters.

For a book on "city," Alexander never actually explains what he or the Bible means by "city" (cf. 15). It is obvious that "city" in English refers, minimally, to a large settlement—a place with a high population density. Yet, it also has further connotations: we juxtapose the city with the country, contrasting urban living with rural living. Contemporary discussion of cities often focuses on their technological nature, and cities have always had significant political connotations. What, though, does a city mean in the Bible?

Alexander never gives an answer to this question. Yet to do so would begin to unveil the great significance of "city." The various Hebrew words

---

[3] All page references are to the pdf digital edition of the book.

translated "city" all have connotations of a large settlement, sometimes with reference to its fortified or politically significant nature. The Greek word usually translated city, *polis*, has specific political connotations. In the passages that Alexander presents, the significance of a city is its relationship to God and his purposes. Consider Babel, it is a city defined by its opposition to God, and it is the focal point of humanity united in opposition to God. In a word, it is the physical embodiment of that kingdom that aligns itself in opposition to God.

Jerusalem, on the other hand, is the physical embodiment of the Kingdom of God, the locus of both his presence and of his rule on earth. At its best, Jerusalem represents the unity of redeemed humanity in the service of God. The focus of city as a theological theme in the Bible is, therefore, not the contrast between rural and urban or technological and natural. Instead, city concerns the embodiment of God's rule and his presence over a people in a specific location (or the antithesis of this).

Following this line thinking, one does not then have to struggle to explain how the figure of the New Jerusalem in Revelation could describe a literal city (cf. 151-152). If a city concerns God's rule and presence among and through a people in a specific location, the conclusion of many commentators and theologians that the New Jerusalem is the redeemed people of God living in the New Creation coheres perfectly with the theme of city. New Jerusalem is a city but not primarily an urban centre: it is the centre of God's political and religious presence on earth among a people united in his kingdom. A high density of people implies a complex infrastructure and thus urbanization, yet this is probably not the focus of the theme of city in Scripture. Though this review is not the place, one could draw from such an understanding of city many implications for the contemporary church and its commission to radiate the glory of God in this world.[4] Such a discussion of city would go a long way to increasing the

---

[4] E.g. J. Alexander Rutherford, "Biblical Themes That Define Us (1): Two Kingdoms," *Teleioteti*, November 1, 2017, accessed May 30, 2019, https://teleioteti.ca/2017/11/01/biblical-themes-that-define-us-two-kingdoms/; "Biblical Themes That Define Us (2): Priests, Soldiers, and Servants," *Teleioteti*, November 8, 2017, accessed May 30, 2019, https://teleioteti.ca/2017/11/08/biblical-themes-that-define-us-2-priests-soldiers-and-servants/; "Biblical

applicability of Alexander's work.

Conclusion

Though I argue that there is something significant missing from *The City of God and the Goal of Creation*, this does not undermine its value. The theme of the City of God touches upon some of the most beautiful promises in Scripture—living in the presence of God and experiencing joy there forevermore!—and will therefore encourage the reader greatly. Furthermore, it will be useful for anyone looking for a place to start in studying the concept of "city" in the Bible and would be helpful for someone intrigued by the appearance of the New Jerusalem in Revelation and curious about its biblical precedent. This is in addition to what was already observed above. Alexander's work is not entirely satisfactory, yet I do not hesitate to recommend it to the reader desiring a concise summary of the theme of city in Scripture; I pray that it would whet your appetite for diving further into the treasures of Scripture's teaching in this regard.

Themes That Define Us (3): Elect Exiles," *Teleioteti*, November 15, 2017, accessed May 30, 2019, https://teleioteti.ca/2017/11/15/biblical-themes-that-define-us-3-elect-exiles/; "Biblical Themes That Define Us (4): Jesus's Family," *Teleioteti*, November 22, 2017, accessed May 30, 2019, https://teleioteti.ca/2017/11/22/biblical-themes-that-define-us-4-jesuss-family/; J. Alexander Rutherford, "Christians and the World: The Ethics of a City on a Hill," *Teleioteti*, November 29, 2017, accessed May 30, 2019, https://teleioteti.ca/2017/11/29/christians-and-the-world-the-ethics-of-a-city-on-a-hill/.

APPENDIX 4: REVIEW OF LIVING IN GOD'S TWO KINGDOMS[1]

One of the most important theological and pastoral issues today—and throughout Church history—is the so-called "Christ and Culture" debate, or how do Christians and the Christian Church relate to the unbelieving world and institutions that are not the church. A dominate stream among Reformed and Evangelical Protestantism today is "transformationalism" or Niebuhr's "Christ the transformer of Culture," the view that Christians are called to transform unbelieving culture into a Christian culture of some sort. Over against this trend, there has been a resurgence of Two-Kingdoms or "Christ and culture in paradox." Meredith Kline and Westminster Seminary California have been particularly associated with a Reformed two kingdoms theory. In his book *Living in God's Two Kingdoms*,[2] David VanDrunen presents a relatively up-to-date defence of this position (published 2010). VanDrunen offers a careful and clear presentation of the doctrine, so the volume is a helpful contribution for the student, pastor, or scholar seeking to understand the main argument for and implications of the Reformed Two Kingdoms doctrine (R2K). Even for the reader who does not sympathize with this position, there are insights to be gleaned; VanDrunen's analysis of

---

[1] VanDrunen, *Living in God's Two Kingdoms*.

[2] I read the Logos edition, which was of good quality except for several paragraphs of text where the footnote was transposed into the body, near the end of the book

the ethic of the Sermon on the Mount as an inversion of the *lex talionis*, instead of giving proportionate retribution it is rendering proportional kindness and mercy in response to injustice, is profound: "When the citizens of heaven refuse to retaliate against an evildoer, but instead endure the second evil themselves, they are a living exhibit of the gospel" (111). However, as for the proposal itself, VanDrunen fails to convince on several grounds. After summarizing the book and VanDrunen's argument, I will then offer an evaluation of VanDrunen's R2K proposal.

Summary

In the first chapter, after discussing the Christ and culture debate, he defines culture as he will use employ it: "In a book such as this, I do not use the term 'culture' in an overly precise or technical way. I use it primarily to refer to the broad range of activities—scientific, artistic, economic, etc.—in which human beings engage" (32). The following six chapters are divided across three parts. The first part, chapters two and three, sketches the biblical-theological context for the Two Kingdoms doctrine, focusing on the contrast between the first Adam and Jesus Christ, the second Adam. These two chapters have a significant role in his case for the R2K doctrine. His argument here is against the continuing cultural mandate, a transformationalist teaching. He argues that Adam's task was probationary, to keep and guard the garden as a test to see if he will inherit the "world-to-come." Because Jesus Christ fully succeeds in Adam's task, securing the world-to-come for Believers who are found in him, there is no task left to accomplish. The rest in the world-to-come that was Adam's ultimate destiny—which he failed to attain—is attained by us in Christ. Therefore, the mandate is no longer valid. For this reason, there is no specific, redemptive task involving general "cultural" duties. This is primarily a negative argument: if the cultural mandate is not in place, transformationalism is false.

The second part, chapters four and five, go through the Old and New Testament, showing how the two kingdoms play out across the Testaments. He argues that there is a spiritual antithesis in play, an essential Reformed doctrine, but contends that this antithesis does not override the cultural commonality ordained in God's common kingdom. The common kingdom is grounded in God's covenant with Noah. This covenant concerns cultural activity, not religious activity, which is associated with God's redemptive covenant. This latter covenant is instituted with Abraham and concerns salvation, "opening up the gates of the world-to-come" (84). The common kingdom is governed by God through nature (e.g. 153-154, 168),[3] the redemptive kingdom is ruled by God through his verbal revelation. In the Old Testament, we see the two kingdoms doctrine working out in Abraham's life, Israel's life outside the land, and Israel's exile in Babylon. Within the land, there is only the redemptive kingdom. In the New Testament, the exilic or sojourner theme in 1 Peter, Hebrews, and elsewhere demonstrates the continuity between these experiences.

The third part, chapters six and seven, zooms in to consider the concrete application of the two kingdoms for the Christian life. VanDrunen argues that Christians should do not have distinctly "Christian" vocations and do not engage in "redemptive" work. Common kingdom work is blessed by God but has no enduring significance, so we live within this kingdom in a "detached" manner. Education is another instance of a common kingdom endeavour. VanDrunen argues that politics is a common kingdom matter; Christian can participate in government, military, or law enforcement. VanDrunen argues that the Bible gives five general principles concerning government by which Christians ought to conduct their common kingdom lives. VanDrunen's focus in this chapter, however, is the Church. He argues that the primary referent of the Church in the New Testament is the local Church *gathered* (116, 132-135): "I distinguish between the work and life of the Church and the work and life of individual believers (or groups of believers) as they make their way in this world. Believers and groups of believers do not constitute 'the church' in everything they do." (117) "Participation in the life of the church, not participation in the cultural activities of the broader world, is central for the Christian life" (133).[4] he argues for the ministerial authority of the Church and the regulatory principle of worship.

---

[3] VanDrunen, *A biblical Case for Natural Law*, 37–39.

[4] VanDrunen, "Bearing Sword in the State, Turning Cheek in the Church: A Reformed Two-Kingdoms Interpretation of Matthew 5:38–42," 329–331.

Evaluation

I love the emphasis on the local Church in *Living in God's Two Kingdoms*. I too am convinced that this is the primary focus of Scripture and the locus of God's work in the world. However, in VanDrunen's discussion here, the same ambiguities and lack of clear biblical warrant that mark the rest of the book become evident. After observing some general tensions and difficulties in the overall proposal of the book, I want to then address the weakness of its biblical-theological foundation in the first 11 chapters of Genesis.

General Weaknesses

The first general weakness in the proposal is its failure to give a *reason* or *hope* to common kingdom endeavours. That is, in the Old Testament, civil life was a faithful service to God to see his rule established on earth. In the New Testament, I would contend, there is an emphasis on the role that "common life" has in upholding the Church's mission.[5] transformationalists find value in everyday activities by connecting common life directly with God's kingdom unfolding on earth. VanDrunen rejects this view but can only say that God has blessed this labour, so it is worthwhile. He writes, "Hard work, with God's blessing, is truly its own reward" (189). I do not think this is the biblical teaching; I am thankful it is not, for this is hardly an encouragement to those who are currently struggling to work hard, to find pleasure in hard work. For those to whom work has not yet proved to be "its own reward," what hope can a pastor, friend, or mentor offer? This doctrine gives no more hope than the world does.

Second, his discussion of the "church" is inadequate. The New Testament indeed focuses on the local Church, but what is not clear is that in the New Testament it is the local Church *gathered* that is the focus. Indeed, most of the instructions to the churches in the New Testament is for the Church dispersed, concerning how Christians live their day-to-day life. Indeed, I do not think there is a clear teaching of the "church" in VanDrunen's proposal. On the one hand, if I am right in understanding the

---

[5] E.g. in Ephesians 4:28, the former thief is called to work with his hands in order that he might have something "to give."

locus of the redemptive kingdom and its ethic in VanDrunen's proposal to be the local Church gathered, how do we make sense of the fact that the Sermon on the Mount and most of the ethical instructions of the New Testament address with how Christians interact with one another and the outside world throughout the week? On the other hand, if I am reading him wrongly and the Church is not just the Church gathered, how does this compute with the Two Kingdom's Doctrine? How can Christians have a political theory (*a common kingdom* theory) based in Scripture? If Scripture speaks to the non-redemptive sphere, how can one maintain that they are so distinct after all? VanDrunen clarifies elsewhere that Scripture illumines natural law;[6] however, in this regard, it is not clear from the biblical teaching concerning the so-called common kingdom that these teachings are grounded in or able to be derived from a "natural law."

Third, he does not deal adequately with the challenges Neo-Calvinists have raised with natural law. He affirms that there is no "neutral ground," the foundational tenant of the spiritual antithesis. But if this is the case, then what foundation is there for the common kingdom? That is, if Christians acknowledge certain common domains from *Scripture*, how can someone argue the same things from the common perspective? It is hard to distinguish family and state, state and education, etc. on the basis of common reason alone. Furthermore, there has been a great number of works in the last century that have shown that there is no coherent foundation of ethical reasoning—or reasoning at all—apart from the existence of God and his spoken word.[7] How can we live in the common kingdom when we do not share a system of rationality or ethics with those with whom we are we are supposed to share this kingdom? We may distinguish and share with the world a view that certain institutions are not strictly religious, "Family," "state," etc. Yet, our understanding of each institution will lose its similarity the moment we dig deeper; the commonality is on the surface alone.

There is, of course, common grace, yet this is only an explanation for why we experience agreement between believers and unbelievers; common grace is not a sufficient ground for a common reason or coherent natural

---

[6] VanDrunen, "Two Kingdoms and Moral Standards."

[7] Rutherford, *The Gift of Knowing*.

law.[8] I do not think Romans 1-2 is a sufficient foundation for natural law, for here the revelation is of God himself and those who receive it quickly distort this revelation and interpret the creation in the categories of the Creation. This is an incoherent starting point that hardly allows for shared rational discourse. The point is this: if God has established a common kingdom, it's nature and institutions and basic moral boundaries are not clearly discernible, and the ability to rationally maintain a belief in and knowledge of these structures is not clear. It is not clear that we have the ability to live consistently in that world apart from verbal revelation. This need not pose a problem for Christians, for VanDrunen fails to give a sufficient exegetical foundation for believing God has established a common kingdom.

Exegetical Foundations

VanDrunen's single argument against the continuing creation mandate is that this mandate has as its end the world-to-come which Jesus perfectly attains. Therefore, because Jesus has perfectly attained it, there is no continuing mandate. The first problem with this argument is that there is no exegetical reason anywhere in the first three chapters of the Bible, or the Old Testament, to believe that the creation mandate has as its goal "the world-to-come." The one passage VanDrunen turns to is Hebrews 2.[9] Here the author writes, "For it was not to angels that God subjected the world to come" (2:5). The author of Hebrews quotes after this from Psalm 8, a psalm about creation. However, the author of Hebrews point is that Jesus is the one who truly reigns, in fulfilment of the God's initial instructions to humanity through Adam, and that this reign will be consummated in "the world to

---

[8] In this regard, common grace is God's act to restrain unbelievers from rejecting the truth entirely; otherwise, they would have no truth at all. This implies that what rationality possessed by the unbelieving world is inconsistent rationality. It is rationality that holds onto God's truth while explicitly rejecting the one who makes it true. Though this is often considered an act of common grace, the only biblical text I can find in support is Romans 1, which suggests that unbelieving humans have some truth not because God restrains them but because they go so far as to attribute what is true about God to his creation. It is their idolatry that allows them to enjoy some sort of rational life. However, God restraining judgment is definitely an act of common grace.

[9] he does argue the parallel with God's rest on day seven, but that could be interpreted dozens of different ways

come." This "world to come" is itself ambiguous, for it is already inaugurated through Christ yet not fully arrived.[10] The author does not argue that this is clear from Genesis nor from Psalm 8. The fact that we *now* see that the "world to come" is the locus of this consummated reign does not mean that we can read this back into Genesis: to do so is to reject the gradual unfolding of revelation across the canon and the history it records. A much clearer reading of Genesis is that God commissioned Adam to spread his kingdom on earth as his representative king. However, Adam failed in this mission; God's kingdom would now spread in a world enthralled in rebellion. Only in the New Testament do we learn that this kingdom will be fully inaugurated at Christ's return—something about which the apostles showed great confusion (e.g. Acts 1:6). For these reasons, VanDrunen's rejection of the cultural mandate simply does not follow.

Furthermore, when we trace the creation mandate (or better, the kingdom mandate) throughout Scripture, we see that continues but in a transformed form.[11] Noah is again instructed to rule and multiply, yet like Adam, he sins. With Abraham, we see the echoing of ruling and multiplying (Genesis 12), yet God says that he will now accomplish this Kingdom purpose. In the Torah, we see the provisions for this earthly kingdom of God mandated (e.g. Deuteronomy 17). Yet when the king does arrive, the kingdom is pushed off into the future (2 Samuel 7). The kingdom mandate appears in the New Testament, but in a transformed form: in Matthew 28, we are told the Christ now has dominion, yet his people are commissioned with spreading this rule through throughout the world—with being fruitful and multiplying. The mandate has been accomplished by Christ, but it needs to be worked out in history by his people. However, the mandate at this point looks nothing like the original mandate—a point on which I agree with VanDrunen over against the transformationalists. If the cultural mandate has been transformed in this regard, then there is clearly no clear division between "cultural" and NT "kingdom" actions. We also see in addition to this kingdom mandate an unfolding tension throughout Scripture between

---

[10] As argued in F. F. Bruce, *The Epistle to the Hebrews*, NICNT (Grand Rapids: Eerdmans, 1964); R. T. France, "Hebrews," in *The Expositor's Bible Commentary*, ed. Tremper Longman and David E. Garland, Rev. ed. (Grand Rapids: Zondervan, 2006).

[11] See chapter 5

the Serpent's appropriation of the kingdom mandate, embodied in the historical Babel and symbolic Babylon, and the righteous fulfilment of the mandate through God's covenants.

In line with this, when we get to Genesis 9, the "be fruitful and multiply" language is not simply an affirmation of common kingdom institutions but a reaffirmation of God's kingdom mandate to Noah. Gentry and Wellum argue that the language of the Noahic covenant is explicitly that of a recommission of Adam's original covenant, so we cannot find a unique covenant institution here.[12] Indeed, if the "creation mandate" is a "kingdom mandate," then there is no firm distinction between the Adamic, Noachene, and Abrahamic covenants. They form a continuity of God's single purpose in history, to realize his rule on earth through a Davidic Son in the full unveiling of his glory. Indeed, there is no clear indication of the common institutions to be found in Genesis 9. The "be fruitful and multiply" command is hardly an institution of a structured family unit, and the lex talionis is an instruction for interpersonal retribution, not state-imposed justice. The later developments of these ideas cannot be read into this chapter in an exegetically responsible manner. VanDrunen confesses this when he writes that the authority structures defining common cultural institutions are not found in Genesis 9 but are worked out by the inner logic of these relations. The trouble emerges when we ask, what normative foundation do we have for this inner logic? That a child is dependent on a parent does not clearly indicate, apart from verbal revelation, that the former is subordinate to the later or for how long such subordination should endure. And apart from the verbal *lex talionis*, it is hard to justify the formers indebtedness to the later to be reciprocated in the form of care rendered later in life. This may be why in many modern societies, children abandon this responsibility, for there is no coherent natural logic for this relationship. It is a logic that comes through the revelation of God.

Conclusion

In short, despite the genuinely helpful insights found here or there,

---

[12] Gentry and Wellum, *Kingdom through Covenant*.

VanDrunen's case is neither biblically compelling nor sufficiently robust to deal with the complexities of the Christian life in the contemporary world. This raises a problem, though. I think VanDrunen is right to reject the transformationalist project. However, if my suggestions above are on track, then there are serious problems with the R2K project as well—as many transformationalists have shown (cf. John Frame, *The Doctrine of the Christian Life*). Indeed, VanDrunen does not address several key texts for formulating a doctrine of Christian life in the world. For example, Daniel and Revelation both portray this world as a place of cosmic warfare between God's kingdom and the demonic kingdoms that set themselves in opposition to his purpose. From this perspective, Christians endure amid this conflict until Christ brings it to an end. Also, in 2 Corinthians 6, Paul uses the Levitical doctrine of physical separation to illustrate Christian spiritual separation from unbelievers; if this is rightly applied to marriage (as VanDrunen's one reference to this text affirms), then it surely applies to business, political, and other common kingdom relationships that bring Christians into a unity of purpose with unbelievers and with Satan's kingdom expressed through them. Anabaptists attempt to capture this latter idea with a doctrine of physical separation, but Reformed theologians of various persuasions are agreed in their rejections of this position. What this suggests is that each of the major positions articulated by Reformed Christians and the broader Evangelical world have good things to say but are incorrect in their overarching claim. God willing, I hope to articulate a vision of cultural engagement in a forthcoming book that takes the insights of each of these positions—and others—seriously within a biblical theological framework of God's kingdom unfolding through the Church in history with its consummation at Christ's return.

BIBLIOGRAPHY

Adams, Jay Edward. "Christian Education : A Three-Walled Enterprise. (Editorial)." *Journal of Pastoral Practice 1979* (January 1, 1979).

Alexander, T. Desmond. *The City of God and the Goal of Creation.* Short Studies in Biblical Theology. Wheaton: Crossway, 2018.

Aristotle. "Metaphysics." In *The Works of Aristotle*, edited by W. D. Rose and J. A. Smith. Vol. 8. Logos Edition. Oxford: The Clarendon Press, 1908.

Augustine, Saint. *Saint Augustine: The City of God.* Translated by Gerald G. Walsh and Mother Grace Monahan. Vol. 7. The Fathers of the Church: The Writings of Augustine 14. Washington, D.C.: The Catholic University of America Press, Inc., 1981.

Ayres, Lewis. *Nicaea and Its Legacy: An Approach to Fourth-Century Trinitarian Theology.* 1st ed. Oxford: Oxford University Press, 2004.

Bahnsen, Greg L. *Van Til's Apologetic: Readings and Analysis.* Phillipsburg: P&R Publishing, 1998.

Bauckham, Richard. *Jude, 2 Peter.* Waco, Tex.: Word Books, 1983.

Beale, G. K. *A New Testament Biblical Theology: The Unfolding of the Old Testament in the New.* Grand Rapids: Baker Academic, 2011.

Beale, G.K. *The Book of Revelation: A Commentary on the Greek Text.* NIGTC. Grand Rapids; Carlisle: Eerdmans; Paternoster, 1999.

Behr, John. *The Nicene Faith: Vol 2 of Formation Of Christian Theology.* Crestwood, N.Y.: St Vladimir's Seminary Press, 2004.

———. *The Way to Nicaea.* The formation of Christian theology v. 1. Crestwood, N.Y.: St. Vladimir's Seminary Press, 2001.

Berkhof, Louis. *Systematic Theology.* Grand Rapids: Eerdmans, 1996.

Boersma, Hans. *Heavenly Participation: The Weaving of a Sacramental Tapestry.* Grand Rapids: Eerdmans, 2011.

———. *Sacramental Preaching: Sermons on the Hidden Presence of Christ.* Grand Rapids: Baker Academic, 2016.

Boettner, Loraine. "Postmillennialism." In *The Meaning of the Millennium: Four Views*, edited by George Eldon Ladd and Robert G. Clouse. Downers Grove: InterVarsity Press, 1977.

Brown, Peter Robert Lamont. *The World of Late Antiquity, AD 150-750.* New York: W.W. Norton, 2013.

Bruce, F. F. *The Epistle to the Hebrews.* NICNT. Grand Rapids: Eerdmans, 1964.

Calvin, John. *Commentaries on the Epistles of Paul the Apostle to the Corinthians.* Translated by John Pringle. Bellingham: Logos Bible Software, 2010.

Carson, D. A. *Christ and Culture Revisited.* Grand Rapids; Cambridge: Eerdmans, 2008.

Chester, Tim. *Truth We Can Touch: How Baptism and Communion Shape Our Lives.* Wheaton, Illinois: Crossway, 2020.

Chesterton, G. K. *Orthodoxy.* Kindle. London: William Clowes and Sons LTD, n.d.

Clark, Gordon H. *Thales to Dewey: A History of Philosophy.* Cambridge, Massachusetts: The Riverside Press, 1957.

Dempster, Stephen G. *Dominion and Dynasty: A Biblical Theology of the Hebrew Bible.* New Studies in Biblical Theology 15. Leicester: Downers Grove: Apollos; InterVarsity, 2003.

Dockery, David S., and Christopher W. Morgan, eds. *Christian Higher Education: Faith, Teaching, and Learning in the Evangelical Tradition.* Wheaton: Crossway, 2018.

Dreher, Rod. *The Benedict Option: A Strategy for Christians in a Post-Christian Nation.* New York, New York: Sentinel, 2017.

Foster, M. B. "The Christian Doctrine of Creation and the Rise of Modern Natural Science." *Mind* 43, no. 172 (1934): 446–468.

Foster, M.B. "Christian Theology and Modern Science of Nature (Part 1)." *Mind* 44 (1935): 439–466.

———. "Christian Theology and Modern Science of Nature (Part 2)." *Mind* 45 (1936): 1–27.

Frame, John M. *A History of Western Philosophy and Theology.* Phillipsburg: P&R Publishing, 2015.

———. *Cornelius Van Til: An Analysis of His Thought.* Phillipsburg: P&R Publishing, 1995.

———. *The Doctrine of the Christian Life.* A Theology of Lordship 4. Phillipsburg: P&R Publishing, 2008.

Frame, John M. "The Institutes of Biblical Law: A Review Article." *The Works of*

John Frame and Vern Poythress. Accessed May 17, 2020. https://frame-poythress.org/the-institutes-of-biblical-law-a-review-article/.

France, R. T. "Hebrews." In *The Expositor's Bible Commentary*, edited by Tremper Longman and David E. Garland. Rev. ed. Grand Rapids: Zondervan, 2006.

Gentry, Peter John, and Stephen J. Wellum. *Kingdom through Covenant: A Biblical-Theological Understanding of the Covenants*. Wheaton: Crossway, 2012.

Goldsworthy, Graeme. *The Goldsworthy Trilogy*. Milton Keynes: Paternoster, 2012.

Guinness, Os. *The Global Public Square: Religious Freedom and the Making of a World Safe for Diversity*. InterVarsity Press, 2013.

Hoekema, Anthony A. *The Bible and the Future*. Revised, Reprint. Grand Rapids: Eerdmans, 1994.

Holland, Tom. *Dominion: How the Christian Revolution Remade the World*. First US edition. New York: Basic Books, 2019.

Hollmann, Joshua. "Christian Witness in the Present: Charles Taylor, Secularism, and The Benedict Option." *Concordia Journal* 46, no. 1 (2020): 57–67.

J. Alexander, Rutherford. "Review of Truth We Can Touch." *Teleioteti*, April 27, 2020. Accessed May 13, 2020. https://teleioteti.ca/2020/04/27/review-of-truth-we-can-touch/.

Johnson, Alan F. "Revelation." In *Hebrews - Revelation*, edited by Tremper Longman III and David E. Garland. Rev. ed. The Expositor's Bible Commentary. Grand Rapids: Zondervan, 2006.

Keller, Timothy. *Center Church: Doing Balanced, Gospel-Centered Ministry in Your City*. Grand Rapids: Zondervan, 2012.

Kline, Meredith G. "Kingdom Prologue," 1993.

Lake, Kirsopp, trans. *The Apostolic Fathers*. Cambridge MA; London: Harvard University Press, 1912.

Leeman, Jonathan. *One Assembly: Rethinking the Multisite and Multiservice Church Models*. 9marks. Wheaton, Illinois: Crossway, 2020.

Niebuhr, H. Richard. *Christ and Culture*. New York: Harper Torchbooks, 1951.

Nietzsche, Friedrich Wilhelm, and Walter Kaufmann. *Basic Writings of Nietzsche*. Modern Library ed. New York: Modern Library, 2000.

Plantinga, Cornelius. *Engaging God's World: A Christian Vision of Faith, Learning, and Living*. Grand Rapids: Eerdmans, 2002.

Plato. *The Republic: English Text*. Edited by T. E. Page, E. Capps, W. H. D. Rouse, L. A. Post, and E. H. Warmington. Cambridge, MA; London: Harvard University Press; William Heinemann Ltd., 1937.

Poythress, Vern Sheridan. *Logic: A God-Centered Approach to the Foundation of Western Thought*. Electronic. Wheaton: Crossway, 2013.

Rushdoony, Rousas J. *The Institutes of Biblical Law*. 3 vols. Phillipsburg: P & R Pub, 1973.

Rutherford, J. Alexander. *Believe the Unbelievable: A Study in Habakkuk*. Teleioteti Study Guides 1. Vancouver, BC: Teleioteti, 2018.

———. "Biblical Themes That Define Us (1): Two Kingdoms." *Teleioteti*, November 1, 2017. Accessed May 30, 2019. https://teleioteti.ca/2017/11/01/biblical-themes-that-define-us-two-kingdoms/.

———. "Biblical Themes That Define Us (2): Priests, Soldiers, and Servants." *Teleioteti*, November 8, 2017. Accessed May 30, 2019. https://teleioteti.ca/2017/11/08/biblical-themes-that-define-us-2-priests-soldiers-and-servants/.

———. "Biblical Themes That Define Us (3): Elect Exiles." *Teleioteti*, November 15, 2017. Accessed May 30, 2019. https://teleioteti.ca/2017/11/15/biblical-themes-that-define-us-3-elect-exiles/.

———. "Biblical Themes That Define Us (4): Jesus's Family." *Teleioteti*, November 22, 2017. Accessed May 30, 2019. https://teleioteti.ca/2017/11/22/biblical-themes-that-define-us-4-jesuss-family/.

———. "Christians and the World: The Ethics of a City on a Hill." *Teleioteti*, November 29, 2017. Accessed May 30, 2019. https://teleioteti.ca/2017/11/29/christians-and-the-world-the-ethics-of-a-city-on-a-hill/.

———. "Faith Comes through Hearing, and Hearing through the Word of Christ: The Centrality of Scripture in the Early Presbyterian Missions to Korea (1884-1910)." Teleioteti, 2017.

———. *God's Kingdom through His Priest-King: An Analysis of the Book of Samuel in Light of the Davidic Covenant*. Teleioteti Technical Studies 1. Vancouver: Teleioteti, 2019.

———. "Review of From Chaos to Cosmos." *Teleioteti*, December 12, 2018. Accessed March 23, 2020. https://teleioteti.ca/2018/12/12/review-of-from-chaos-to-cosmos/.

———. "Review of Media, Journalism, and Communication." *Teleioteti*, May 10, 2018. Accessed March 25, 2020. https://teleioteti.ca/2018/05/10/review-of-media-journalism-and-communication/.

———. "Review of One Assembly." *Teleioteti*, May 25, 2020. Accessed June 7, 2020. https://teleioteti.ca/2020/05/25/review-of-one-assembly/.

———. "Review of The City of God and the Goal of Creation." *Teleioteti*, March 8, 2018. Accessed March 24, 2020. https://teleioteti.ca/2018/03/08/review-of-the-city-of-god-and-the-goal-of-creation/.

———. *The Book of Habakkuk: An Exegetical-Theological Commentary on the Hebrew Text.* A Teleioteti Old Testament Commentary 1. Vancouver, BC: Teleioteti, 2019.

———. *The Gift of Knowing: A Biblical Perspective on Knowing and Truth.* God's Gifts for the Christian Life Part 1 Vol. 1. Vancouver: Teleioteti, 2019.

———. *The Gift of Reading - Part 1: Reading the Bible in Submission to God.* God's Gifts for the Christian Life Part 1 Vol. 2a. Vancouver: Teleioteti, 2019.

Rutherford, James. "Benefits of Secularity." *The Gospel Coalition | Canada*, n.d. Accessed May 17, 2020. https://ca.thegospelcoalition.org/article/benefits-of-secularity/.

Rutherford, Samuel. *Lex, Rex, or the Law and the Prince.* Edinburgh: R. Ogle, 1843.

Sayers, Dorothy. "The Lost Tools of Learning- Dorothy Sayers." *Association of Classical Christian Schools (ACCS)*, January 5, 2017. Accessed June 6, 2020. https://classicalchristian.org/the-lost-tools-of-learning-dorothy-sayers/.

Schaeffer, Francis A. *The Great Evangelical Disaster.* Westchester: Crossway Books, 1984.

Schuchardt, Read Mercer. *Media, Journalism, and Communication: A Student's Guide.* Reclaiming the Christian Intellectual Tradition. Wheaton: Crossway, 2018.

Singer, C. Gregg. "A Philosophy of History." In *Jerusalem and Athens: Critical Discussions on the Theology and Apologetics of Cornelius Van Til*, edited by E. R. Geehan. Phillipsburg: Presbyterian and Reformed Publishing Co., 1971.

Stark, Rodney. *The Rise of Christianity: A Sociologist Reconsiders History.* Princeton University Press, 1996.

Steinmetz, David C. "The Superiority of Precritical Exegesis." In *A Guide to Contemporary Hermeneutics: Major Trends in Biblical Interperation*, edited by Donald K. McKim. Grand Rapids: Eerdmans, 1986.

Turner, David L. *Matthew.* Baker Exegetical Commentary on the New Testament. Grand Rapids: Baker Academic, 2008.

Van Til, Cornelius. *A Christian Theory of Knowledge.* Philadelphia: Presbyterian and Reformed Pub Co., 1969.

———. *An Introduction to Systematic Theology.* In Defense of the Faith V. Presbyterian and Reformed Pub. Co., 1974.

———. *Essays on Christian Education.* Phillipsburg: The Presbyterian and Reformed Publishing Company, 1979.

———. "Part 3--A. The Dilemma of Education." In *Essays on Christian Education.*

Phillipsburg: The Presbyterian and Reformed Publishing Company, 1979.

———. *The Defense of the Faith*. Edited by K. Scott Oliphint. 4th ed. Phillipsburg: P & R Pub, 2008.

Van Til, Henry R. *The Calvinistic Concept of Culture*. Grand Rapids: Baker Book House, 1959.

VanDrunen, David. *A Biblical Case for Natural Law*. The Action Institute, 2006.

———. "Bearing Sword in the State, Turning Cheek in the Church: A Reformed Two-Kingdoms Interpretation of Matthew 5:38–42." *Themelios* 34, no. 3 (2009).

———. *Divine Covenants and Moral Order: A Biblical Theology of Natural Law*. Emory University studies in law and religion. Grand Rapids: Eerdmans, 2014.

———. *Living in God's Two Kingdoms: A Biblical Vision for Christianity and Culture*. Crossway, 2010.

———. "Two Kingdoms and Moral Standards." College. *Valiant for Truth*, February 28, 2011. https://web.archive.org/web/20120122080308/http://wscal.edu/blog/entry/two-kingdoms-and-moral-standards.

Veith, Gene Edward. *Post Christian: A Guide to Contemporary Thought and Culture*. Wheaton: Crossway, 2020.

Waltke, Bruce K., and Charles Yu. *An Old Testament Theology: An Exegetical, Canonical, and Thematic Approach*. 1st ed. Grand Rapids: Zondervan, 2007.

Wilson, Douglas. *Empires of Dirt: Secularism, Radical Islam, and the Mere Christendom Alternative*. Moscow, Ida.: Canon Press, 2016.

———. *The Case for Classical Christian Education*. Wheaton: Crossway Books, 2003.

Wright, N. T. *Surprised by Hope: Rethinking Heaven, the Resurrection, and the Mission of the Church*. 1st ed. New York: HarperOne, 2008.

Zachhuber, Johannes. *The Rise of Christian Theology and the End of Ancient Metaphysics: Patristic Philosophy from the Cappadocian Fathers to John of Damascus*. Oxford University Press, 2020.

"How Do I Find a Good Church?" *Desiring God*. Last modified February 7, 2020. Accessed May 14, 2020. https://www.desiringgod.org/interviews/how-do-i-find-a-good-church.

"What Should I Look for in a Church?" *9Marks*. Accessed May 14, 2020. https://www.9marks.org/answer/what-should-i-look-church/.

ABOUT TELEIOTETI

Teleioteti (Τελειοτητι, te-ley-o-tey-tee)—meaning "unto maturity"—is dedicated to faithful, thoughtful ministry. We create resources for Christian discipleship, resources that address theological and pastoral concerns from a biblical worldview. Our purpose is to see Christ's Church mature in its understanding of God and his Word. We do this through the production of Gospel-centred materials that connect the Bible with the heads, hearts, and minds of Christians. We hope to enable Christians from all walks of life to better understand and glorify God through service in his Church.

To achieve this purpose, Teleioteti publishes online materials and books researched with academic rigour yet based upon biblical presuppositions. That is, we are neither academic nor lazy. We use methods, or epistemology, informed by the Bible along with the hard work usually associated with professional research and study. We produce resources directed towards all Christians, but most of our resources are directed towards students, pastors, and theologically inclined lay Christians.

To learn more about us and what we are doing, please visit us at https://teleioteti.ca or contact us at info@teleioteti.ca. If you have found this resource helpful, prayerfully consider supporting us by giving a review on the web (e.g. Amazon, Goodreads, etc.), praying with and for us, or giving financially so that we can produce more resources like this one. For more information on how you can support us, visit us at https://teleioteti.ca/about/partner/.

Other Books by J. Alexander Rutherford

Other books in this series, "God's Gifts for the Christian Life" include the three volumes of Part 1 The Christian Mind (Volumes 1 and 2 are currently available, Volume 3 is in the process of writing). For all of our books, visit Teleioteti.ca. For upcoming books, see our page, Teleioteti.ca/coming-soon/.

Believe the Unbelievable: A Study in the Book of Habakkuk (Teleioteti, 2018)

What would we do if our prayers for justice, our prayers that God's will be done in our nation, were answered with a vision of desolation, of utter destruction?

When Habakkuk prayed for salvation, a prayer for justice in the midst of chaos, violence, and suffering, that was God's answer. He revealed in a vision the invasion of the vicious armies of Babylon. God's answer contradicted everything Habakkuk thought he knew. Yet in the end, he praised God and trusted him for this horrid salvation.

What do we do when God's actions or words contradict our understanding, contradict what we have believed? The book of Habakkuk answers this question in the face of the Babylonian invasion of Judah. Habakkuk is a book of discipleship, a book written to bring its reader to a deeper faith in Yahweh in the presence of his unthinkable deeds.

Using study questions addressing the text, theology, and application of Habakkuk and explanatory comments on difficult themes, *Believe the Unbelievable* seeks to realize this purpose for the contemporary reader.

Endorsements:

James Rutherford is a capable and creative thinker, well equipped to tackle tough projects, such as the book of Habakkuk. In this study guide, Rutherford has produced a very useful resource for individual or group study. He combines theological acumen and well-honed linguistic and literary skills to discover and then to present, in highly understandable fashion, the riches of this not so "minor" Minor Prophet.

- V. Philips Long, PhD Cambridge
    Professor of Old Testament, Regent College

My good friend, James Rutherford, has given the church a gift. He has taken his love for God's Word and focused it on an Old Testament book that most Christians know very little about. The result is a study in Habakkuk that brings together deep insight and real relevance. Habakkuk is a voice among the biblical chorus that believers need to hear today. Thank you, James, for helping us to hear it clearly and faithfully.

- Fredrick Eaton
    Pastor, Christ City Church, Kitsilano

Prevenient Grace: An Investigation into Arminianism – 2ⁿᵈ Revised Edition (Teleioteti, 2020)

When a building is built on a poor foundation, the inevitable result is its collapse. But this isn't a book on architecture; foundations are found in thought structures as well as in material structures. In theology, a bad foundation will produce results as catastrophic as a bad foundation in architecture. How we think about God and his work in the world will profoundly affect how we live and work out our Christian faith; is your foundation strong? This book evolved from the conviction that a prominent theological system rests on a fragile foundation.

Endorsements:

This book is a fine piece of scholarship. Rutherford presents his arguments with admirable clarity. His intention is to offer guidance for pastors and teachers who may be faced with questions about whether human beings have the freedom to accept or reject God. The great strength of Rutherford's book is his knowledge of biblical texts and an appropriate interpretation of them. He successfully shows that the claims of Arminianism with its view that prevenient grace allows an acceptance or rejection of God are not supported by biblical texts. Nor are they justified by philosophical arguments. They layout of the book and its careful treatment of arguments both for and against prevenient grace is a model of excellent writing. His chapters are supplemented by a Glossary that explains all specific terms and Appendices where detailed theological discussions are given. Most helpful is his Index of Scripture passages discussed.

- Dr. Shirley Sullivan
    FRSC (elected), Professor Emeritus of Classics, University of British Columbia

www.ingramcontent.com/pod-product-compliance
Lightning Source LLC
Chambersburg PA
CBHW021445070526
44577CB00002B/270